Financial Fitness for Life

Bringing Home the Gold
Grades 9-12

Teacher Guide

John S. Morton
Mark C. Schug

NCEE

National Council on Economic Education

Authors:

John S. Morton is Vice President for Program Development at the National Council on Economic Education. Previously, he was a classroom teacher for 30 years and served as President of the Arizona Council on Economic Education. He has written numerous articles and publications in economic education.

Mark C. Schug is Director of the Center for Economic Education and Professor of Curriculum and Instruction at the University of Wisconsin-Milwaukee. He has taught for over 30 years at the middle school, high school, and university levels and has written widely in economic education.

Project Director:

John E. Clow is the Director of the Leatherstocking Center for Economic Education at the State University of New York, College at Oneonta and Professor Emeritus of that college. He is a national award-winning college teacher, speaker, and author in the fields of personal finance, economics, and business education.

Design:
Roher/Sprague Partners

This publication was made possible through funding by the Bank of America Foundation.

ISBN 1-56183-546-3   5 4 3 2 1

TABLE OF CONTENTS

TABLE OF CONTENTS

9-12

Lesson is appropriate for all students in 9-12 grade levels.

Lesson may be challenging for some students in 9-12 grade levels.

ACKNOWLEDGEMENTS

The members of the writing team express their sincere appreciation to the many individuals who were involved with this project.

Reviewers:

Jody Hoff, *Senior Vice President & Program Administrator*
Idaho Council on Economic Education
Boise State University
Boise, Idaho

Don R. Leet, *Director*
Center for Economic Education
California State University—Fresno
Fresno, California

State council directors who coordinated the field-testing:

R. J. (Jim) Charkins, California Council on Economic Education, San Bernardino, California

Donald G. Fell, Florida Council on Economic Education, Tampa, Florida

David L. Ramsour, Texas Council on Economic Education, Houston, Texas

Teachers, students, and parents involved in field-testing in California, Florida, and Texas.

General Editor:

Richard Western
Milwaukee, Wisconsin

Some materials were adapted from *Wallet Wisdom*, a 1996 publication of the National Council on Economic Education, by Janet H. Bishop (Principal Writer), Deborah Mackey, and Vickie L. White. The publication was underwritten by a consortium of 10 Consumer Credit Counseling Services (CCCS) Agencies.

FOREWORD

For more than 50 years, the National Council on Economic Education (NCEE) has been calling attention to the need to educate our young people effectively in the skills of economics and personal finance and showing how that need can best be met. These new materials for teachers, sponsored by the Bank of America Foundation, provide an excellent and dramatic step in the direction of improving economic and financial literacy.

NCEE is proud of this splendid partnership with the Bank of America Foundation—and of the product.

We have found that students exposed to the economic way of thinking are more self-confident and more competent in making financial decisions, building their careers, and acting as informed citizens. By gaining understanding of the "real" world, we increase our prospects for better lives. Thanks to this distinctive program, we can now improve substantially on that kind of learning-for-life for millions of young people—who are our future.

NCEE's new multifaceted, comprehensive, and integrated program addresses the issue of economic and financial illiteracy by offering teaching-learning materials at four levels—grades K-2, 3-5, 6-8, and 9-12. There are 15 to 22 lessons in each part. Content for each of the grade levels is based on the *Voluntary National Content Standards for Economics*, which NCEE wrote and published, as well as the national guidelines for personal finance. Lessons are geared to active learning with games, simulations, role-playing, and computer use. All of the materials are also correlated with the extensive educational tools in personal finance and economics on our web site: **www.ncee.net**.

One exciting feature of these outstanding materials is that, for the first time, NCEE is offering parent guides for each educational level. Our research shows that students learn a considerable amount of their economic decision-making abilities from their parents. So NCEE is committed to assisting parents in the practical education of their children. These guidebooks are fun, as well as informative and instructive, for both students and their parents.

Nationally recognized experts in personal finance and economic education wrote the materials. Other experts and practitioners in the field reviewed them. The materials were then field-tested in three states over a period of two months. Each lesson was used by at least six teachers in urban, suburban, and rural settings. Refinements were made in the lessons according to the reviews from the field-testing.

We are proud of the results—which will now become the leading edge of personal finance education for all students K-12.

Our thanks go to many people for this important development. Without the visionary philanthropy of the Bank of America Foundation, this project would not have been possible. We are also indebted to the authors of each set of documents; their dedication, insight, and creativity will become immediately apparent to users of these materials in the classroom and at home. We are grateful as well to the reviewers of the materials, and to the teachers, parents, and students in California, Florida, and Texas who field-tested the materials. Finally, and especially, we thank Dr. John E. Clow who directed the developmental work; because he has worked in the vineyard of economic and personal financial education for several decades, his knowledge of the field has been invaluable in orchestrating this significant project.

Robert F. Duvall, Ph.D.
President & Chief Executive Officer
The National Council on Economic Education (NCEE)

INTRODUCTION

The Financial Fitness for Life Curriculum consists of high-quality materials that assist students from kindergarten to grade 12 in making better decisions for earning income, spending, saving, borrowing, investing, and managing their money. The materials at the four levels (grades K-2, 3-5, 6-8, and 9-12) focus on a fitness theme.

Developing financial fitness is like developing physical fitness. Both require developing a knowledge base and then applying it. The development of knowledge for use in the everyday life of the students is a main goal of the lessons. Each level uses a fitness terminology. The headings for the different parts of each lesson include *Equipment* (materials needed), *Warm-up* (introduction to lesson), *Workout* (body of lesson), and *Cool Down* (summary and review). An analogous concept also stressed in the materials is that one must continually work on financial fitness, just as with physical fitness, because of new developments. The materials emphasize, though, that some basic routines are used consistently in order to maintain financial fitness, such as the importance of determining the cost of each choice and the realization that there is no free lunch.

Besides the fitness focus, some other features are common to all of the levels. They include:

1. Each set of materials is based on **national standards**. Matrices show how the materials relate to the national standards for economics and the national guidelines for personal finance.

2. All materials employ economics, called **the science of decision making**, as a way to prioritize the staggering array of choices facing students when they make decisions. By prioritizing, students learn how to make better decisions, and, equally important, to avoid poor ones. The emphasis on using economic concepts and an economic way of thinking distinguishes these materials from other materials used to develop personal financial literacy. The economic concepts and economic ways of thinking are basic fitness routines used when a person deals with personal financial matters.

3. Active learning and student reflection on these activities dominate all materials. Active learning without reflection does not necessarily enhance true learning defined as changing behavior. Active learning *plus* reflection optimizes true learning. As with physical fitness, one must "do" and then "reflect" upon what one did in order to incorporate that learning into one's lifestyle.

4. Developing physical fitness involves doing a variety of exercises and varying those exercises over time. Similarly, these materials include a variety of methods that appeal to many different learning styles. Role playing, group discussions, gathering information from the Internet, reading materials, interviewing individuals, drawing pictures, and analyzing case problems are some of the many teaching methods that are found in the materials. Even more materials are available on the web site of the National Council on Economic Education **(www.ncee.net)** to add to the repertoire of activities and materials.

5. A number of influential coaches can enhance the fitness process, especially when developing financial fitness. Parents as partners in the educational process are an integral part of this set of materials. Parents play an important role in developing the personal financial literacy of their children because of the modeling that they do in everyday life. The lesson plans for each educational level have a parent guide, which provides background information and fun activities for both the parent and the child.

6. Similar to planning physical fitness activities for different ages, the economic and personal finance concepts are approached at the experiential/developmental level of the student. More abstract applications of economic and personal finance concepts are found at the higher educational levels than at the lower ones. The developmental approach to learning has been a hallmark of National Council on Economic Education (NCEE) materials for several decades.

Using the Teacher Guide for **Bringing Home the Gold**

THE 22 LESSONS in the 9-12 document are divided into five theme areas—the economic way of thinking, earning an income, saving, spending and borrowing, and managing money. Most of the lessons are estimated to take one class period; some may take up to two class periods. The lessons in each theme area can be used sequentially; each can also be used alone.

THE STUDENT WORKOUTS include reading materials relating to the content of a lesson in addition to worksheets to promote active, reflective learning. An introductory section focuses on what is covered in the theme area. Major concepts of the theme are addressed, not through a descriptive narrative, but through Frequently Asked Questions.

The Parents' Guide has activities that parents can do with their sons and daughters. *The Parents' Guide* includes content, worksheet activities, other activities, and resources. It is recommended that a guide be provided for each family. A letter to the parents from the teacher will help gain their cooperation. A reminder of when the parents should do a specific activity would be beneficial in developing this school/home educational partnership. Encourage this educational partnership by having students report either orally or in writing on the activities they do with their parents.

High school students enjoy learning about personal finance because it involves making decisions about their lives. Generally, high school students have an excellent readiness to develop financial literacy because they are looking forward to living "on their own" in the near future. They want to know some strategies to use to make their income go as far as it can. Personal finance is an interdisciplinary area where language arts, computation, economics, finance, reasoning, and decision making are all brought together. We hope that you, your students, and their parents will enjoy the learning activities in these lessons and find them to be exciting, enriching experiences about some very important facts and skills for life.

John E. Clow, Ed.D.
Project Director
Financial Fitness for Life

Claire Melican
Vice President for Program Administration
National Council on Economic Education

TABLE 1 Correlation of **Bringing Home the Gold** Lessons with the National Standards for Economics*

⬇ Standards/Lessons ➡	1	2	3	4	5	6	7	8	9	10	11	12	13	14	15	16	17	18	19	20	21	22
1. Scarcity		✔	✔																			
2. Marginal costs/ marginal benefits		✔	✔					✔			✔	✔			✔	✔	✔					
3. Allocation of goods and services																						
4. Role of incentives		✔																				
5. Gain from trade		✔									✔											
6. Specialization and trade																						
7. Markets – price and quantity determination																						
8. Role of price in market system																						
9. Role of competition																						
10. Role of economic institutions											✔		✔						✔	✔		
11. Role of money																						
12. Role of interest rates		✔									✔			✔								
13. Role of resources in determining income	✔	✔		✔		✔																
14. Profit and the entrepreneur	✔			✔	✔																	
15. Growth																						
16. Role of government							✔											✔				

* Taken from Voluntary National Content Standards in Economics, *National Council on Economic Education (NCEE), 1997.*

TABLE 2   Correlation of **Bringing Home the Gold** Lessons with the National Personal Finance Management Guidelines*

Lessons 12-21 on next page

⬇ Guidelines/Lessons ➡	1	2	3	4	5	6	7	8	9	10	11
A. INCOME											
1. Determinants of income	✔	✔		✔		✔					
2. Sources of income		✔		✔	✔	✔					
3. Taxes and transfer payments							✔				
B. MONEY MANAGEMENT											
4. Opportunity cost		✔	✔					✔			
5. Short and long term financial goals									✔		✔
6. Budgeting											
7. Relationship between taxes, income, spending, and financial investment								✔			
8. Risk management								✔	✔	✔	✔
9. Personal financial responsibility											✔
10. Perform basic financial operations											
C. SPENDING AND CREDIT											
11. Spending now versus spending later	✔										
12. Costs and benefits of multiple transactions instruments											
13. Risk and credit											
14. Credit history and records											
15. Rights and responsibilities of buyers, sellers, and creditors											
16. Choosing among spending alternatives											
17. Managing financial difficulties											
D. SAVING AND INVESTING											
18. Saving now versus saving later								✔	✔		
19. Short- and long-term saving and investment strategies	✔							✔	✔	✔	
20. Evaluate alternative investment decisions								✔	✔		
21. Impact of government policies on saving and investment decisions											

TABLE 2 CONTINUED

↓ Guidelines/Lessons ➡	12	13	14	15	16	17	18	19	20	21	22
A. INCOME											
1. Determinants of income											
2. Sources of income											
3. Taxes and transfer payments											
B. MONEY MANAGEMENT											
4. Opportunity cost									✔		
5. Short- and long-term financial goals									✔		
6. Budgeting									✔		
7. Relationship between taxes, income, spending, and financial investment											
8. Risk management											✔
9. Personal financial responsibility	✔	✔						✔			
10. Perform basic financial operations		✔	✔	✔	✔	✔	✔		✔	✔	
C. SPENDING AND CREDIT											
11. Spending now versus spending later	✔									✔	
12. Costs and benefits of multiple transactions instruments											
13. Risk and credit	✔										
14. Credit history and records		✔									
15. Rights and responsibilities of buyers, sellers, and creditors	✔							✔	✔		
16. Choosing among spending alternatives				✔	✔	✔					
17. Managing financial difficulties											
D. SAVING AND INVESTING											
18. Saving now versus saving later	✔										
19. Short- and long-term saving and investment strategies											
20. Evaluate alternative investment decisions											
21. Impact of government policies on saving and investment decisions											

* Taken from Personal Financial Management Guidelines and Benchmarks, *Jump$tart Coalition for Personal Financial Literacy, 1998.*

THEME

1

There Is
No Such Thing
as a Free Lunch

O V E R V I E W

This first unit introduces students to the topics of personal finance, economics, and consumer decision making.

Lesson 1

is a quiz game on the characteristics of millionaires and successful strategies for becoming a millionaire. The lesson is designed to grab the students' attention and give them reasons for studying personal finance. Another goal is to have fun.

Lesson 2

introduces the students to the concept of scarcity and an economic way of thinking. Students use the *The Handy Dandy Guide* to see how two families with identical circumstances can have very different levels of wealth.

Lesson 3

focuses on a five-step decision-making model and a decision-making grid. This model will be useful as the students learn about making decisions regarding education, spending, saving, investing, and credit.

1

LESSON

1

How to Really Be a Millionaire

Fitness Focus

EQUIPMENT
AND GETTING READY!

Make transparencies of the Visuals.

✔ Theme 1 *Student Letter* and *Frequently Asked Questions (Bringing Home the Gold Student Workouts)*

✔ Visual 1.1, *The Millionaire Game*

✔ Visual 1.2, *Rules for Improving Your Financial Life*

✔ Exercise 1.1, *The Millionaire Game Score Sheet (Bringing Home the Gold Student Workouts)*

✔ Family Activity 1, *Find Your Family Economic Literacy IQ (The Parents' Guide to Bringing Home the Gold)*

✔ An 8 1/2" x 11" sheet of paper with a large "T" printed on one side and a large "F" printed on the other side for each student group

✔ An 8 1/2" x 11" sheet of paper with "Millionaire" printed on it for each group'

LESSON DESCRIPTION

This lesson is designed to get students interested in personal finance. Financial planning may seem dull and laborious, but finding out how to become a millionaire is an activity that tends to stir up considerable interest. This lesson shows the students that they are unlikely to achieve wealth without self-discipline. Achieving personal wealth involves planning and making sound choices, such as getting a good education, spending wisely, saving early and often, and taking prudent risks. The lesson here is not that the only goal in life is to become rich. Wealth, in itself, is no guarantee of happiness. Nevertheless, wealth provides the freedom to have more choices in life.

TIME REQUIRED 1 class period.

This lesson is correlated with national standards for economics as well as the national guidelines for personal financial management as shown in Tables 1 and 2 in the front of the book.

Student Objectives

At the end of this lesson the student will be able to:

✔ Describe the characteristics of millionaires.

✔ Illustrate how sound financial decisions can increase wealth and a person's standard of living.

2

PARENT CONNECTION

Family Activity Worksheet 1 in *The Parents' Guide* focuses on having at least one of your students' parents take the economic test of financial literacy. It's fun and they don't have to bring it back to school.

The Parents' Guide is a tool for reinforcing and extending the instruction provided in the classroom. It includes:

1. Content background in the form of frequently asked questions.

2. Interesting activities that parents can do with their young adults.

3. An annotated listing of books and Internet resources related to each theme.

Workout

WARM-UP

A. Tell the students that the purpose of this lesson is to show how they can make choices that can improve their lives. The lesson has several tips about the accumulation of personal wealth. It introduces ideas that will be explored throughout the study of economics and personal finance.

B. Have the students read the Student Letter and the FAQs for Theme 1 in *Workouts*. Discuss the answers to the questions.

Answers to the Student Letter Questions

1. How much do high school students know about personal finance and economics? (*Not much. On two major national tests, the average score was an F.*)

2. What is personal finance? (*Learning how to manage your money wisely.*)

3. Is there a payoff for learning personal finance? (*Yes, it can make you wealthier.*)

EXERCISE

A. Divide the class into groups of three. To each group, distribute one sheet of paper with "T" on one side and "F" on the other, and one sheet with "Millionaire" written on it.

B. Explain the rules of the *Millionaire Game.*

1. Choose a spokesperson for each group.

2. All students in the group must tell the spokesperson what they think the right answers are for the questions on Visual 1.1.

3. The majority prevails whenever the group disagrees on the answer.

4. The spokesperson must hold up the sheet of paper with "T" and "F" to indicate the group's decision on the question. A team must answer each question. The spokesperson must also hold up the

"Millionaire" sign if the group wants to use this option.

5. Each group gets five points for each correct answer. Each group loses five points for each incorrect answer.

6. Each group may choose to "Millionaire" on any question up to a total of five questions. If the group answers correctly, it receives 10 points; if the group answers incorrectly, it loses 10 points from its current score. Groups should use this tactic on questions they are most confident about answering correctly.

7. A total of 100 points is a perfect score. To earn this score, the students must answer all questions correctly and "Millionaire" correctly on five questions.

8. The team with the most points wins and is declared The Millionaires of Tomorrow.

C. Display Visual 1.1, *The Millionaire Game*, on the overhead projector. At first, keep all the questions covered. Show the students one question at a time so they do not see them all at once.

D. For each question, ask the students to decide in their group if they think the statement is true or false. Then the spokesperson holds up the "True/False" sign to show the group's decision to the class. The spokesperson should also hold up the "Millionaire" sign if this tactic was chosen for this question. Make sure these sheets are raised simultaneously to discourage some groups from waiting to see what other groups decided. Or the groups can write their answers to all the questions first and then calculate their score.

E. While the students keep track of their scores on Exercise 1.1 in *Student Workouts*, keep a point total on the board so that each group can see how it is performing relative to other groups. They will use this information to decide when to go "Millionaire."

F. Discuss the answers as the students answer each question or at the end of the game. Explain to the students some basic principles for getting rich and living a more satisfying life.

　1. *True. Four of five millionaires are college graduates. Eighteen percent have Master's degrees, eight percent law degrees, six percent medical degrees, and six percent Ph.D.s.*

　2. *False. About 2/3 of millionaires work 45-55 hours a week.*

　3. *True. Only 19 percent of millionaires received any income or wealth of any kind from a trust fund or an estate. Fewer than 10 percent of millionaires inherited 10 percent or more of their wealth.*

　4. *False. Only 28.6 percent of millionaires have American Express Gold Cards while 43 percent have Sears credit cards. Only 6.2 percent of millionaires have American Express Platinum Cards.*

　5. *True. Ford is preferred by 9.4 percent and Cadillac by 8.8 percent. Lincoln comes in third at 7.8 percent. Only 23 percent of millionaires drive a current-year (new) car.*

　6. *False. A majority of millionaires are in ordinary industries and jobs. They are proficient in targeting marketing opportunities.*

　7. *False. About three out of four millionaires are self employed and consider themselves to be entrepreneurs. Most of the others are professionals, such as doctors, accountants, and lawyers.*

　8. *False. Few people get rich the easy way. If you play the lottery, the chances of winning are about one in 12 million. The average person who plays the lottery every day would have to live about 33,000 years to win once. In contrast, you have a one in 1.9 million chance of being struck by lightning. A pregnant woman has one chance in 705,000 births to have quadruplets. How many sets of quadruplets do you know?*

　9. *True. In recent years, the average college graduate earned 66 percent more than the average high school graduate did. People with professional degrees earned 150 percent more than high school graduates did.*

　10. *True. Of course, a normal person would spend some of the difference, but it is a dramatic illustration of how valuable a high school diploma is. The difference in earnings between a high school graduate and a high school dropout is $8000 at age 18. The illustration assumes the difference increases by 1.5 percent each year and that the difference is invested at eight percent interest each year.*

　11. *False. Recent studies show that 80 percent of day traders lose money.*

　12. *False. Long term (starting in 1926 and including the Great Depression), the Standard & Poor's 500 Stock Index has increased at about an 11 percent compound annual rate of return, exceeding the return on any other investment. Of*

Financial Fitness for Life: Bringing Home the Gold Teacher Guide, ©National Council on Economic Education

course, there is risk. The stock market has down years, and there is no guarantee of an 11 percent return in the future, especially in the short run. In contrast, the long-term return on risk-free U.S. government securities during the same period ranged from five to six percent. The actual return depended on the term of the bond. Another way of looking at this is that $1.00 invested in the S&P 500 on January 1, 1926, was worth $1,828 on December 31, 1997. One dollar invested in long-term government bonds during the same period was worth $39 on December 31, 1997. It probably paid to take the additional risk of buying stocks.

13. *True. Because of the power of compound interest, small savings can make a difference. It pays to resist temptation and live below your means.*

14. *True. Because of the power of compound interest, the earlier you begin saving, the better. Regular saving will make you a millionaire, even if your salary is modest.*

15. *False. Most millionaires are married and stay married. By contrast, divorce is a gateway to poverty. Financially speaking, divorce is something you want to avoid, particularly after you have children. It is important to choose a marriage partner carefully.*

G. At the end of the game, display Visual 1.2, *Rules for Improving Your Financial Life*, and go over the principles. Show that these rules are derived from the answers to the questions in the Millionaire Game.

COOL DOWN

A. Have the students write a brief essay on "How to Really Become a Millionaire."

B. The answers to this test come primarily from two excellent sources:

- Lee, Dwight R., and Richard B. McKenzie. *Getting Rich in America.* Harper Business, 1999.
- Stanley, Thomas J., and William D. Danko. *The Millionaire Next Door.* Pocket Books, 1996.

Other Training Equipment

An annotated bibliography and Internet resource list are available on our web site, **www.ncee.net**, as well as in *The Parents' Guide to Bringing Home the Gold.*

5

Visual 1.1

The Millionaire Game

Answer each question "True" or "False." For each correct answer, you will receive five points. For each incorrect answer, you will lose five points. For any five questions, you may hold up the "Millionaire" sheet with your answer. If you answer correctly, you will receive 10 points. If you answer incorrectly, you will lose 10 points.

1 Most millionaires are college graduates.

2 Most millionaires work fewer than 40 hours a week.

3 More than half of all millionaires never received money from a trust fund or estate.

4 More millionaires have American Express Gold Cards than Sears cards.

5 More millionaires drive Fords than Cadillacs.

6 Most millionaires work in glamorous jobs, such as sports, entertainment, or high tech.

7 Most millionaires work for big Fortune 500 companies.

8 Many poor people become millionaires by winning the lottery.

9 College graduates earn about 65 percent more than high school graduates earn.

10 If an average 18-year-old high school graduate spends as much as an average high school dropout until both are 67 years old, but the high school graduate invests the difference in his or her earnings at eight percent annual interest, the high school graduate would have $5,500,000.

11 Day traders usually beat the stock market and many of them become millionaires.

12 If you want to be a millionaire, avoid the risky stock market.

13 At age 18, you decide not to smoke and save $1.50 a day. You invest this $1.50 a day at eight percent annual interest until you are 67. At age 67, your savings from not smoking are almost $300,000.

14 If you save $2000 a year from age 22 to age 65 at eight percent annual interest, your savings will be over $700,000 at age 65.

15 Single people are more often millionaires than married people.

Visual 1.2

Rules for Improving Your Financial Life

1. Get a good education.

2. Work long, hard, and smart.

3. Learn money-management skills.

4. Spend less than you could spend.

5. Save early and often.

6. Invest in common stocks for the long term.

7. Gather information before making decisions.

LESSON

2

The Economic Way of Thinking

Fitness Focus

EQUIPMENT AND GETTING READY!

Make a transparency of the Visual.

✔ Visual 2.1, *The Handy Dandy Guide*

✔ Exercise 2.1, *A Mystery of Two Families (Bringing Home the Gold Student Workouts)*

✔ Exercise 2.2 *The Boring School Mystery (Bringing Home the Gold Student Workouts)*

LESSON DESCRIPTION

Lesson 2 introduces students to the economic reasoning process or the "economic way of thinking." Students reason through two situations, using *The Handy Dandy Guide*, a primer on economic reasoning.

This lesson is correlated with national standards for economics as well as the national guidelines for personal financial management as shown in Tables 1 and 2 in the front of this book.

PARENT CONNECTION

There is no specific family activity for this lesson, but there are activities in *The Parents' Guide* that parents might want to use with this lesson. They can be found in the "Raising the Bar" section for Theme 1.

The Parents' Guide is a tool for reinforcing and extending the instruction provided in the classroom. It includes:

1. Content background in the form of frequently asked questions.
2. Interesting activities that parents can do with their young adults.
3. An annotated listing of books and Internet resources related to each theme.

Student Objectives

At the end of this lesson the student will be able to:

✔ List and explain the basic principles of economic reasoning.

✔ Use economic reasoning to explain how improved money-management skills can improve a family's standard of living.

✔ Use economic reasoning to explain why more education results in higher income and more opportunities in the future.

8

Workout

WARM-UP

Explain to students that the purpose of this lesson is to teach them how to use economic reasoning. To achieve this, they will use principles of a device called *The Handy Dandy Guide.*

EXERCISE

A. Use Visual 2.1 to introduce the economic reasoning process to the students.

B. Have the students read Exercise 2.1A, *Mystery of Two Families (Student Workouts).* This could be assigned as homework.

C. Have the students answer the questions at the end of the reading.

D. Go over the answers to the questions.

1. What is an opportunity cost? *(It is the best alternative that a person gives up to get something. The opportunity cost is the second-best option.)*

2. Why is opportunity cost important when you make choices? *(Everything has a cost. By considering costs, you make better decisions.)*

3. Why do people want to be wealthy? *(In order to buy more goods and services in the future, to provide themselves with more freedom of choice, or to use their wealth to help other people.)*

4. What difference does it make if the United States is viewed as a land of victims or a land of opportunities? *(Victims are passive. Taking advantage of opportunities will improve your life.)*

5. What is the incentive for saving? *(Interest.)*

6. Why are the Robinsons wealthier than the Meltons? *(They made better decisions regarding the accumulation of wealth.)*

COOL DOWN

A. Ask the students to read Exercise 2.2, *The Boring School Mystery* in *Workouts.* Have the students get into groups to solve the mystery. The students have been provided a list of clues regarding why students stay in school or leave school. Have each group:

1. Select a spokesperson to report to the class. List the clues that explain why many students stay in school. You could even ask them to rank the clues in order of importance. *(Points 2, 3, 6, 7, and 8 are reasons to stay in school.)*

2. List the clues that explain why some students drop out of school. *(Points 1, 4, and 5 are reasons to drop out.)*

B. Display Visual 2.1, *The Handy Dandy Guide,* to explain why more students stay in school

than drop out. Go over the answers to Exercise 2.2. The answers are:

1. What is the cost of staying in school? *(Lost income from work, activities other than school, homework.)*

2. What is the cost of dropping out of school? *(Lower future income.)*

3. What is the incentive for staying in school? *(Higher future income, a wider choice of jobs, interesting activities, and the opportunity to attend college.)*

4. How does the American economic system encourage people to graduate from high school? *(The United States is a land of opportunities, and an education allows people to take advantage of many more opportunities.)*

9

5. Is going to high school voluntary or do you have no choice? *(After age 16, in most states, it is voluntary.)*

6. Why do some students choose to drop out of school? *(They feel the costs of school are greater than the benefits. They may desire the immediate rewards of higher income or freedom, or they may want to help their family.)*

7. Why do most students choose to stay in high school and graduate? *(The benefits of higher future income and additional future opportunities outweigh the costs of more income and more time now.)*

8. What are the future consequences of a decision to drop out of school or stay in school? *(Dropping out of school will limit future choices; staying in school will expand them.)*

Other Training Equipment

An annotated bibliography and Internet resource list are available on our web site, **www.ncee.net**, as well as in *The Parents' Guide to Bringing Home the Gold.*

Financial Fitness for Life: Bringing Home the Gold Teacher Guide, ©National Council on Economic Education

Visual 2.1

The Handy Dandy Guide

1. People choose.

2. All choices involve costs.

3. People respond to incentives in predictable ways.

4. People create economic systems that influence choices and incentives.

5. People gain when they trade voluntarily.

6. People's choices have consequences for the future.

LESSON

3

Decision Making

Fitness Focus

EQUIPMENT
AND GETTING READY!

Make transparencies of the Visuals.

✔ Visual 3.1, *Five-Step Decision-Making Model*

✔ Visual 3.2, *A Decision-Making Grid*

✔ Exercise 3.1, *Decision Making (Bringing Home the Gold Student Workouts)*

✔ Exercise 3.2, *Personal Decision Making (Bringing Home the Gold Student Workouts)*

✔ Exercise 3.3, *Buying a New P.C. (Bringing Home the Gold Student Workouts)*

✔ Family Activity 2, *How Can We Decide? (The Parents' Guide to Bringing Home the Gold)*

LESSON DESCRIPTION

In this lesson, students learn that we must make decisions because resources are limited and wants are unlimited. Students see that sound decision making involves identifying criteria and using those criteria to make decisions. Students use a decision-making grid to understand how such a grid can be used to choose a college. They then use a similar grid to decide what personal computer to buy.

This lesson is correlated with national standards for economics as well as the national guidelines for personal financial management as shown in Tables 1 and 2 in the front of the book.

PARENT CONNECTION

Family Activity Worksheet 2 in *The Parents' Guide* focuses on having the family use the decision-making grid for making a future decision. The family activity should be assigned after coverage in class as to how to use the decision-making grid. It would be beneficial to have students report on what the students and parents learned from using the grid.

The Parents' Guide is a tool for reinforcing and extending the instruction provided in the classroom. It includes:

1. Content background in the form of frequently asked questions.

2. Interesting activities that parents can do with their young adults.

3. An annotated listing of books and Internet resources related to each theme.

TIME REQUIRED
1 class period.

12

Workout

WARM-UP

Tell the students that a fundamental law of economics is that "there is no such thing as a free lunch." Ask the students to speculate on why this might be true. Explain that this lesson focuses on the concept of scarcity and how we all have to make choices.

EXERCISE

A. Have the students read Exercise 3.1, *Decision Making* in *Student Workouts* and answer the questions about scarcity.

B. Go over the answers to the questions with the class. Be sure the students understand that because of scarcity, they must make sound decisions.

1. Why is there no such thing as a free lunch? *(Because wants are unlimited and resources are scarce, we must make choices.)*

2. Give some examples of natural resources, human resources, and capital resources. *(Examples will vary. Examples of natural resources could include water, oil, minerals; examples of human resources include intelligence, physical strength, education, agility, compassion, sense of humor; capital resources include machinery, buildings, equipment.)*

3. What is capital? *(Goods used to produce other goods and services.)*

4. Why do economists NOT view capital as money? *(Money is used to make the exchange of goods and services easier. Printing more money would just increase prices, not provide people with more goods and services.)*

5. What is an opportunity cost? *(The next best alternative not chosen.)*

C. Display Visual 3.1, *Five-Step Decision-Making Model.* Explain the model as necessary.

Student Objectives

At the end of this lesson the student will be able to:

✔ Describe how scarcity affects economic choices.

✔ Describe and discuss the five-step decision-making model.

✔ Use the decision-making model and decision-making grid to make economic choices.

D. Display Visual 3.2, *A Decision-Making Grid,* and explain how a decision-making grid works. List the alternatives and criteria that students suggest. Evaluate the alternatives by using a -, +, or ++ to indicate how well an alternative meets a criterion. Then encourage students to recommend decisions, noting the trade-offs involved, and how criteria might be weighed differently by different individuals. You might use the grid to make some decisions such as:

• Spending or saving the income from a part-time job.

• Buying a product such as a CD or clothing.

• Deciding whether to study for a test or go to a movie.

E. Have the students read Exercise 3.2, *Personal Decision Making,* and fill in the decision-making grid. Review the plusses or minuses the students choose.

F. Discuss the answers (given on the next page).

13

Maria's Decision-Making Grid

What is the problem? *(Choosing the right college for Maria to attend.)*

ALTERNATIVES	CRITERIA			
	Low Cost	**Quality Program**	**Personal Attention**	**Close to Home**
State U	+	++	-	+
Local Community College	++	+	+	++
Private College	-	++	++	-

What choice do you recommend for Maria based on her criteria?
(To attend Local Community College for two years.)

1. **Why is the decision making model important?** *(It helps a person make better decisions by evaluating the alternatives against the criteria.)*

2. **Are there any additional criteria that Maria did not consider that you feel are important in choosing a college?** *(Possible answers include the social life, the number of friends who are students there, extracurricular activities, and safety of the campus.)*

3. **Do you agree with Maria? Why or why not?** *(Answers will vary because students may not believe each criterion has equal weighting or importance.)*

COOL DOWN

A. Have the students use the decision making grid in Exercise 3.3 to make a decision about buying a personal computer. This exercise should be assigned as homework because students will have to visit stores or use the Internet. You may want to have the students complete this activity in groups or individually.

B. A variation of this activity is to bring advertisements for computers to class so students do not have to visit stores.

C. Another variation is to have the students use information from web sites of computer companies, such as Dell, Gateway, Compaq, and IBM to complete the grid.

Other Training Equipment

An annotated bibliography and Internet resource list are available on our web site, **www.ncee.net**, as well as in *The Parents' Guide to Bringing Home the Gold.*

Financial Fitness for Life: Bringing Home the Gold Teacher Guide, ©National Council on Economic Education

Visual 3.1

Five-Step Decision-Making Model

Step 1.   Define the Problem.

Step 2.   List Your Alternatives.

Step 3.   State Your Criteria.

Step 4.   Evaluate Your Alternatives.

Step 5.   Make a Decision.

Visual 3.2

A Decision-Making Grid

The Problem: _____

_____

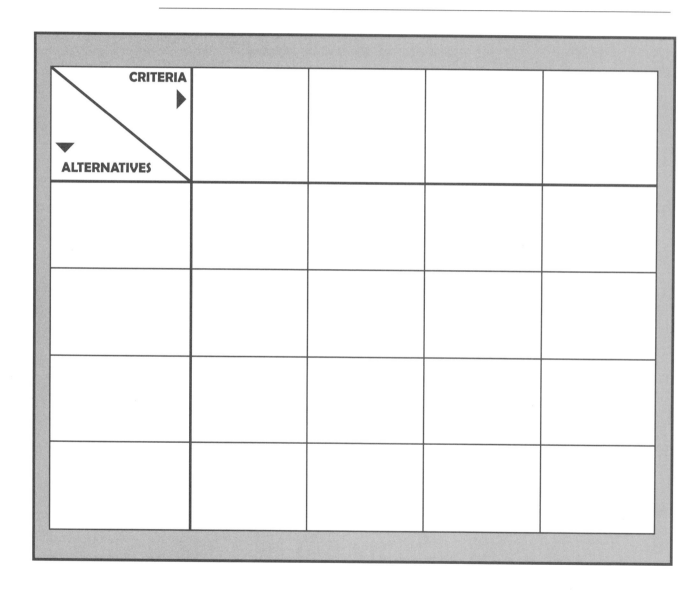

The Decision: _____

_____

THEME 2

Education Pays Off: Learn Something

OVERVIEW

This second unit introduces students to the topics of finding a job, entrepreneurship, and the relationship between increased levels of formal education and income.

Lesson 4

provides an overview of the job-seeking process including finding job openings, writing a letter of application, preparing a resume, and completing an application. Students work in pairs to practice their job-interview skills.

Lesson 5

stresses the idea that not everyone works for someone else. Some people work for themselves. Through an informal attitude survey, students learn about the characteristics of entrepreneurs. The lesson goes on to compare some of the advantages and disadvantages of being an entrepreneur and some potential areas of small business success.

Lesson 6

focuses on why people make different incomes. It points out that while many factors contribute to differences in income, education is one of the most important. Students examine Census Bureau data that illustrate the relationship between level of education and income. The lesson concludes with a game called Capitalizing on Your Human Capital where students learn about the level of education required for various occupations.

Lesson 7

looks at that first paycheck. It introduces students to the differences between gross pay and net pay. It teaches them how to compute simple deductions using tax tables to determine the take-home pay of two fictional employees.

LESSON

4

Job Application Process

Fitness Focus

LESSON DESCRIPTION

Getting a job is fundamental to achieving economic success. Most people begin their work lives working for others. While obtaining a job can be a challenge, there are widely accepted practices in business and government that make the process less difficult. This lesson provides an overview of steps for finding job openings, writing a letter of application, preparing a resume, completing an application, and participating in an interview.

This lesson is correlated with national standards for economics as well as the national guidelines for personal financial management as shown in Tables 1 and 2 in the front of the book.

PARENT CONNECTION

Family Activity Worksheet 3 in *The Parents' Guide* asks the parents and their son or daughter to select an employment ad that interests the student and discuss what it takes to prepare for the selected position. Parents assist their son or daughter to complete a letter of application and resume for the position.

The Parents' Guide is a tool for reinforcing and extending the instruction provided in the classroom. It includes:

1. Content background in the form of frequently asked questions.

2. Interesting activities that parents can do with their young adults.

3. An annotated listing of books and Internet resources related to each theme.

EQUIPMENT
AND GETTING READY!

✔ Theme 2 *Student Letter* and *Frequently Asked Questions* (Bringing Home the Gold Student Workouts)

✔ Exercise 4.1, *The Job Application Process* (Bringing Home the Gold Student Workouts)

✔ Exercise 4.2, *Sample Job Application* (Bringing Home the Gold Student Workouts)

✔ Exercise 4.3, *Job Postings and Interview Forms* (Bringing Home the Gold Student Workouts)

✔ Illustration 4.1, *Sample Letter of Application* (Bringing Home the Gold Student Workouts)

✔ Illustration 4.2, *Sample Resume* (Bringing Home the Gold Student Workouts)

✔ Family Activity 3, *Finding a Job Opportunity (The Parents' Guide to Bringing Home the Gold)*

Workout

WARM-UP

A. Have the students read the student letter and FAQs for Theme 2 and answer the questions.

Answers to the Student Letter Questions

1. What are some of the steps involved in getting a job? *(Writing a letter of application, preparing a resume, completing a job application, and getting a job interview.)*

2. If you want to earn a living, do you have to work for someone else? *(No. You may wish to be an entrepreneur.)*

3. Is there a payoff for investing in your education? *(Yes. Increased levels of formal education are related to earning more income.)*

4. Is your paycheck the total number of hours worked times your rate of pay? *(No, because deductions are made from your gross pay.)*

B. Explain that the purpose of this lesson is to provide students an overview of the steps in the job application process and to give them some opportunities to develop and practice their job-seeking skills.

EXERCISE

A. Have the students read Exercise 4.1, *The Job Application Process* in *Student Workouts* and answer the questions. Discuss the answers.

1. What are the five primary steps of getting a job? *(Look for job openings, write a letter of application, prepare a resume, complete the application, and participate in a job interview.)*

2. What are two suggestions for finding a job? *(Check the America's Job Bank web site offered by the U.S. Department of Labor. Consider ways to network with family, friends, and organizations like the local Chamber of Commerce. Other suggestions are to check with teachers, guidance counselors, local employment agencies, newspaper classified advertisements, and businesses.)*

3. What are two tips for writing a letter of application? *(A letter of application should be a standard business letter. A typical letter expresses your interest in a particular job, links your experience, interest, or training to the job, and explains how you can be reached for an interview.)*

Student Objectives

At the end of this lesson the student will be able to:

✔ Identify the key steps in the job-application process.

✔ Practice job-interview skills.

✔ Practice writing a letter of application and a resume.

4. What information is ordinarily included on a resume? *(Your name, telephone number, street address, e-mail address, career objective, education, work experience, abilities, and other information that might include interests, awards, offices held in organizations, extracurricular activities, and references.)*

19

5. There are many suggestions for how best to conduct yourself at a job interview. Which suggestions do you think are most important? *(Answers will vary but may include: know the company, arrive on time, go alone, dress appropriately, be poised and confident, have a firm handshake, establish eye contact, communicate clearly, be ready for some open-ended questions, emphasize your strong points, and be positive.)*

B. Direct the students' attention to Exercise 4.2, *Sample Job Application* in *Student Workouts*. Ask the students to read through the exercise and answer the questions. Discuss the answers.

1. What information is requested on the job application? *(Personal information such as name, address, and Social Security number, availability to work, and education.)*

2. What are the obligations of individuals with disabilities? *(Individuals with disabilities must inform employers that they need special accommodations.)*

3. What sort of questions are employers not supposed to ask? *(Federal law prohibits hiring decisions being made on the basis of race, color, national origin, religion, gender, pregnancy, marital status, parenthood, age, height, weight, criminal record, or perceived disability. Interviewers and job applications are not allowed to pose personal questions that do not pertain to the requirements of the job.)*

C. Tell the students that they are going to participate in a job-interview simulation. Ask the students who have participated in job interviews to identify some of the characteristics they think employers look for in new employees. List their comments on the board. Some of their suggestions might be that employers seek employees who are punctual, pleasant, courteous, and hard working, have the appropriate skills to do the job, etc.

D. Ask the students to examine Exercise 4.3, *Job Postings and Interview Forms* in *Student Workouts*. Allow the students a few minutes to study the information. Divide the class into pairs. One member of each pair should act as the interviewer and the other should act as the interviewee. Ask one student in each pair to select a job from the Job Postings sheet for which he or she will apply. Ask the other student to use the Interviewer Form to conduct a simulated interview and to complete the evaluator's section. Ask the students to conduct their interviews. When they have completed the first interview, have the students reverse roles so that the interviewer becomes the interviewee and the interviewee becomes the interviewer. At the end of each interview, have the interviewer give the job applicant the completed evaluation form.

E. When the simulated interviews are complete, ask:

• **What questions seem the most difficult for the interviewees to answer?** *(Accept a variety of responses. It is likely that the open-ended questions were the most difficult for the interviewees to answer.)*

• **Which characteristics of the respondent's answers did the interviewers tend to favor?** *(Accept a variety of responses.)*

F. Review some of the key points in this lesson. Ask:

• **What are the five steps in the job-seeking process?** *(Finding job openings, writing a letter of application, preparing a resume, completing an application, and participating in an interview.)*

COOL DOWN

A. Ask the students to visit the web site of the Bureau of Labor Statistics **(www.bls.gov)** and to use the *Occupational Outlook Handbook* to research three jobs of interest to them. They should prepare a report that identifies the occupations they have selected and explain the nature of the work, working conditions, employment, training and other qualifications, plus opportunities for advancement, job outlook, earnings, and related occupations.

B. Ask the students to find a job in which they are interested using the classified ads of the local newspaper or using the web site,

America's Job Bank (**www.ajb.dni.us**). Since most of the jobs in America's Job Bank are full-time, perhaps the local newspaper might be a better source if you want students to consider applying for existing part-time or summer jobs. Direct the students' attention to Illustration 4.1, *Sample Letter of Application,* and Illustration 4.2, *Sample Resume.* Ask the students to prepare a letter of application and a resume for the job they have selected from the newspaper or web site, using the samples in *Student Workouts* as models. The parents are asked to assist their son or daughter with this activity as evidenced by the family activity for this lesson.

Other Training Equipment

An annotated bibliography and Internet resource list are available on our web site, **www.ncee.net**, as well as in *The Parents' Guide to Bringing Home the Gold.*

21

LESSON

5

Making Your Own Job

Fitness Focus

EQUIPMENT AND GETTING READY!

Make transparencies of the Visuals.

✔ Visual 5.1, *Survey Results*

✔ Visual 5.2, *Hear a Business Opportunity Knocking on Your Door?*

✔ Exercise 5.1, *Take the Test (Bringing Home the Gold Student Workouts)*

✔ Exercise 5.2, *Who Are Entrepreneurs? (Bringing Home the Gold Student Workouts)*

✔ Exercise 5.3, *Hear a Business Opportunity Knocking on Your Door? (Bringing Home the Gold Student Workouts)*

✔ Exercise 5.4, *I Wonder Why Nobody Ever Made a... (Bringing Home the Gold Student Workouts)*

✔ 4-5 pieces of poster board and markers for use in the assessment procedure

✔ Small prize for the group with the best commercial in the cool down procedure

LESSON DESCRIPTION

Not everyone works for someone else. Some people make jobs for themselves. They are called entrepreneurs. This lesson focuses on the characteristics of *entrepreneurs,* compares some of the advantages and disadvantages of becoming an entrepreneur, and examines some of the potential areas of success for small business operations.

This lesson is correlated with national standards for economics as well as the national guidelines for personal financial management as shown in Tables 1 and 2 in the front of this book.

PARENT CONNECTION

There is no specific family activity for this lesson, but there are activities in *The Parents' Guide* that parents might want to use with this lesson. They can be found in the "Raising the Bar" section for Theme 2.

Student Objectives

At the end of this lesson the student will be able to:

✔ Recognize the characteristics of entrepreneurs.

✔ Compare the conditions of employment between working for yourself and working for a corporation.

✔ Identify examples of small business opportunities in the areas of service, retail, and franchise, including Internet-related opportunities.

The Parents' Guide is a tool for reinforcing and extending the instruction provided in the classroom. It includes:

1. Content background in the form of frequently asked questions.

2. Interesting activities that parents can do with their young adults.

3. An annotated listing of books and Internet resources related to each theme.

Workout

WARM-UP

Explain that the purpose of this lesson is to help the students identify the characteristics of entrepreneurs and to explore some of the advantages and disadvantages of working for yourself. Many Americans enjoy the challenge of starting up their own businesses. They want to make their own jobs.

TIME REQUIRED 1 class period.

EXERCISE

A. Direct the students' attention to Exercise 5.1, *Take the Test*. Ask the students to complete the questionnaire. Ask the students to total their points from the questionnaire. Tell the students to write their scores anonymously on a small piece of paper. Collect the papers. Display Visual 5.1 on the overhead projector. Record the number of student scores in each of the categories. Stress that this survey is mainly a device to focus the students' attention on some of the key characteristics of people who are entrepreneurs. Discuss the class scores. Ask:

1. **Why do you think students in our class are little inclined, somewhat inclined, inclined, or very inclined toward being entrepreneurs?** *(Accept a variety of answers. Explain that being an entrepreneur is not for the faint of heart or those who are not willing to work hard. There are also rewards in terms of potential income, the chance to make your own decisions, and the satisfaction of starting and sustaining your own business.)*

B. Ask the students to turn to Exercise 5.2, *Who Are Entrepreneurs?* Ask them to read the information and examine the chart, with particular attention to the difference between corporate and small business life. Discuss their answers to the questions.

1. **What are some of the characteristics of entrepreneurs?** *(Entrepreneurs tend to be independent. Among other things, entrepreneurs tend to be confident, hard working, well organized, and self-starters.)*

2. **Is corporate life for you or is running a small business more appealing? Identify three ways in which working in a corporation differs from working for yourself.** *(In a corporation, job stability depends on the success of others as well as employers. In a small business, job stability depends on the owner. In a corporation, work hours are long but predictable. In a small business, work hours are long but determined by the owner. In a corporation, success depends mainly on the success of others. In a small business, success depends on the business. In a corporation, the salary is set in a predetermined range. In a small business, salaries are often low in the beginning but may become very high.)*

In a corporation, there is often a standard benefits package. In a small business, the benefits are up to the owner. In a corporation, job responsibilities are explained in a handbook or in some other fashion. In a small business, the owner is responsible for everything.)

C. Explain to the class that small businesses can be found in every sector of the economy. There are many opportunities for entrepreneurs in the service sector as well as in retail, franchise businesses, and providing services via the Internet. Display Visual 5.2 to the class and ask the students to turn to Exercise 5.3, *Hear a Business Opportunity Knocking on Your Door?* Ask the students to name opportunities in the areas of services to individual households, retail services, franchise, and Internet sales and services that might be important to new entrepreneurs. Please note that these categories may overlap. A completed sample of Visual 5.2 is provided below.

Visual 5.2 Answers (Possible)
Hear a Business Opportunity Knocking on Your Door?

Services to Individual Households	Retail Services	Franchise	Internet Sales and Services
In-home child care	Shoe store	Gas station	Creating web sites
Lawn and tree care	Drug store	Fast food	Book sales
Tutoring	Grocery store	Restaurant	Webmaster
Physical therapy	Restaurant	Hotel	Computer repair
Home repair	Office supply store	Department store	Sports gear
Housekeeping	Florist	Office supply store	Exotic food sales
Delivery service	Pet care	Gourmet coffee shop	Music sales
Shopping service	Hardware store	Employment agency	Radio/television broadcasts
Pet service	Auto parts store	Clothing store	Holiday gift sales
Music lessons	Lumber yard	Eye-care provider	Selling consumer information

Financial Fitness for Life: Bringing Home the Gold Teacher Guide, ©National Council on Economic Education

D. Review some of the key points in this lesson. Ask:

1. **What are some of the key characteristics of an entrepreneur?** *(Risk taker, hard worker, high energy level, achieves results by individual effort, creative, works independently, confident, versatile, finds making money rewarding.)*

2. **What are some of the advantages of being an entrepreneur compared to working in a corporation?** *(The entrepreneur is his or her own boss, which means there is more freedom than one might expect as a corporate employee. There is a possibility of earning much higher income as an entrepreneur compared to working in a corporation.)*

3. **What are some of the disadvantages of being an entrepreneur?** *(Risks, responsibilities, and the hard work can be daunting.)*

COOL DOWN

A. Ask the class to turn to Exercise 5.4, *I Wonder Why Nobody Ever Made a ...?* Divide the class into small groups and ask them to complete the questions in this section. When they are done, ask each group to present its commercial illustrating the good or service to their potential customers—the members of the class. You may wish to give a small prize to the group(s) with the best commercials.

Other Training Equipment

An annotated bibliography and Internet resource list are available on our web site, **www.ncee.net**, as well as in *The Parents' Guide to Bringing Home the Gold.*

Visual 5.1

Survey Results

Score	Category	Number of Students
1-9	Little inclination toward being an entrepreneur.	
10-19	Somewhat inclined toward being an entrepreneur.	
20-29	Inclined toward being an entrepreneur.	
30-40	Very inclined toward being an entrepreneur.	

Visual 5.2

Hear a Business Opportunity Knocking on Your Door?

Services to Individual Households	Retail Services	Franchise	Internet Sales and Services
In-home child care	Shoe store	Gas station	Creating web sites
Lawn and tree care	Drug store	Fast food	Book sales

Financial Fitness for Life: Bringing Home the Gold Teacher Guide, ©National Council on Economic Education

LESSON

6

Why Some Jobs Pay More Than Others

Fitness Focus

LESSON DESCRIPTION

Why do some people earn more income than others? This lesson explains what income is and focuses on how investments in human capital can contribute to increased income. The lesson culminates with an activity linking levels of education to the fastest-growing occupations.

This lesson is correlated with national standards for economics as well as the national guidelines for personal financial management as shown in Tables 1 and 2 in the front of the book.

PARENT CONNECTION

Family Activity Worksheet 4 in *The Parents' Guide* is specifically geared to this lesson. It should be completed prior to the last day of this two-day lesson so that the students are better prepared to write an essay on investing in their own human capital. The activity involves having the parent interview the son or daughter as to the lifestyle that he or she wants as an adult and the steps that will be needed to achieve that lifestyle.

The Parents' Guide is a tool for reinforcing and extending the instruction provided in the classroom. It includes:

1. Content background in the form of frequently asked questions.

2. Interesting activities that parents can do with their young adults.

3. An annotated listing of books and Internet resources related to each theme.

EQUIPMENT AND GETTING READY!

✔ Activity 6.1, *Fastest-Growing Occupations and Level of Education.* Cut into strips

✔ Exercise 6.1, *Why Some Jobs Pay More Than Others (Bringing Home the Gold Student Workouts)*

✔ Exercise 6.2, *Education and Training (Bringing Home the Gold Student Workouts)*

✔ Family Activity 4, *Career Interview (The Parents' Guide to Bringing Home the Gold)*

✔ Six plain sheets of 8.5" x 11" paper for each small group

✔ A small prize for the winning teams

TIME REQUIRED
2 class periods.

28

Workout

WARM-UP

Explain that the purpose of this lesson is to help the students understand why some people earn more income than others. One type of income refers to wages and salary paid to workers in exchange for their work. Another type of income includes money received for use of property. The lesson stresses the importance of investing in your own human capital as a way of increasing individual income.

Student Objectives

At the end of this lesson the student will be able to:

✔ Identify key terms such as income and human capital.

✔ Recognize the relationship between investing in human capital and income.

EXERCISE

A. Ask the students to name people they think have high incomes. List some names on the board. Refer to the first paragraph of Exercise 6.1 *(Student Workouts)* and note the wealth and income of well-known business people and celebrities as well as other people in more conventional occupations such as teachers and cosmetologists.

B. Have the students complete reading Exercise 6.1, *Why Some Jobs Pay More Than Others* and answer the questions. Discuss the answers.

1. **What is income?** *(The wages and salary that a person receives in exchange for work or use of property is called income.)*

2. **What factors other than education contribute to an increased income from work?** *(Demand for the occupation, natural ability, hard work, getting along with others and self-discipline.)*

3. **What is human capital?** *(Human capital is investing in people primarily through education and training.)*

4. **Examine Table 1. Describe the relationship between education and income from work. Does education pay?** *(Higher levels of formal education are associated with higher levels of income.)*

5. **In 1998, how much more would a high school graduate expect to earn per year than an 11th-grade dropout?** *($26,325 - $19,643 = $6,682 more.)*

6. **Assuming a 40-year work life and no pay increases, how much more might a high school graduate expect to earn over a lifetime than an 11th-grade dropout?** *($6,682 x 40 years = $267,280 more.)*

7. **Does it pay to stay in school one more year and graduate? Why?** *(Yes, because each year of work is at a higher level of income than would be the case without a high school diploma.)*

8. **In 1998, how much more would a college graduate expect to earn per year than a high school graduate?** *($42,695 - $26,325 = $16,370 more.)*

9. **Assuming a 40-year work life and no pay increases, how much more might a college graduate expect to earn than a high school graduate over a lifetime?** *($16,370 x 40 years = $654,800 more.)*

10. **Is education a good investment?** *(Yes. Most people with higher levels of education will earn higher incomes.)*

29

C. Direct the students' attention to Exercise 6.2, *Education and Training* in *Student Workouts.* Ask them to answer the questions. Discuss the answers.

1. What three levels of formal education and training are associated with the fastest-growing jobs? *(Associate's degree, bachelor's degree, and doctoral degree.)*

2. What three levels of training are associated with slower-growing jobs? *(Work experience, long-term on-the-job training, and moderate-term on-the-job training.)*

D. Tell the class that some occupations are growing at faster rates than others. Explain that the amount of education required for these faster-growing jobs varies. Explain the different levels of education including vocational training (less than a 2-year vocational degree), associate's degree (2-year degree), bachelor's degree, master's degree, doctoral degree, and professional degree.

E. Cut apart Activity 6.1, *Fastest-Growing Occupations and Level of Education,* into strips and place the strips in a cup or other container in the front of the room.

F. Tell the class that you are going to play a game called "Capitalizing on Human Capital." The purpose of the game is for students to learn the amount of formal education required for the country's fastest-growing occupations. Divide the class into four or five teams. Give each team six sheets of 8.5" x 11" paper. Tell the students to write one of the following abbreviations on each sheet of paper. The letters should be large enough so that you can read them from the front of the room.

- VT for vocational training
- AD for associate's degree
- BA for bachelor's degree
- MA for master's degree
- DD for doctoral degree
- PD for professional degree

G. Explain that you will pull a slip of paper out of the container and read the occupation that is listed. (The slips of paper with the answers are in Activity 6.1.) Each team should discuss what level of formal education they predict is required. After a minute or two, ask for the teams to raise the sheet of paper showing the level of education they predict is required. Read their predictions out loud. Tell the class the correct answer. Discuss briefly why the indicated level of education is the *usual* requirement for the selected occupation. Give teams five points for each correct answer. Play until one or more teams reaches 25 points. Give the winning team a small prize.

COOL DOWN

A. Review some of the key points in this lesson. Ask:

1. What is income? *(Money paid to individuals in exchange for work or use of property.)*

2. What is human capital? *(Human capital is investing in people primarily through education and training.)*

3. What is a key advantage of investing in human capital? *(People with higher levels of formal education tend to earn higher incomes.)*

B. Explain to the class that people often invest in diverse assets such as stocks, bonds, mutual funds, rental properties, and so forth. Ask the students to write an essay titled "Why Investing in My Human Capital Is in My Portfolio."

Financial Fitness for Life: Bringing Home the Gold Teacher Guide, ©National Council on Economic Education

Other Training Equipment

An annotated bibliography and Internet resource list are available on our web site, **www.ncee.net**, as well as in *The Parents' Guide to Bringing Home the Gold.*

ACTIVITY 6.1

Fastest-Growing Occupations and Level of Education

Cut the rectangles below into strips. Place the strips into a container for use during the Capitalizing on Human Capital game. The game calls for you to draw slips out of the container, read the occupation, ask students to predict the level of education required, and then read the amount of education that is generally required.

Source: U.S. Bureau of Labor Statistics, 2000

Occupation: Veterinarian *Education: Professional degree*	Occupation: Computer systems analyst *Education: Bachelor's degree*
Occupation: Physician *Education: Professional degree*	Occupation: Database administrator *Education: Bachelor's degree*
Occupation: Lawyer *Education: Professional degree*	Occupation: Physician's assistant *Education: Bachelor's degree*
Occupation: Biologist *Education: Doctoral degree*	Occupation: Computer support specialist *Education: Associate's degree*
Occupation: Physicist *Education: Doctoral degree*	Occupation: Paralegal *Education: Associate's degree*
Occupation: College professor *Education: Doctoral degree*	Occupation: Physical therapy assistant *Education: Associate's degree*
Occupation: Speech-language pathologist *Education: Master's degree*	Occupation: Health information technician *Education: Associate's degree*
Occupation: Physical therapist *Education: Master's degree*	Occupation: Data processing equipment repairer *Education: Postsecondary vocational training*
Occupation: Urban planner *Education: Master's degree*	Occupation: Surgical technologist *Education: Postsecondary vocational training*
Occupation: Curator *Education: Master's degree*	Occupation: Emergency medical technician *Education: Postsecondary vocational training*
Occupation: Computer engineer *Education: Bachelor's degree*	Occupation: Manicurist *Education: Postsecondary vocational training*

LESSON 7

Uncle Sam Takes a Bite

Fitness Focus

EQUIPMENT
AND GETTING READY!

Make transparencies of the Visuals.

✔ Visual 7.1, *Key for Paycheck #1*

✔ Visual 7.2, *Key for Paycheck #2*

✔ Exercise 7.1, *What Are All These Deductions from My Paycheck? (Bringing Home the Gold Student Workouts)*

✔ Exercise 7.2, *Calculating a Paycheck #1 (Bringing Home the Gold Student Workouts)*

✔ Exercise 7.3, *Calculating a Paycheck #2 (Bringing Home the Gold Student Workouts)*

✔ Table 7.1, *Federal Tax Table (Bringing Home the Gold Student Workouts)*

✔ Table 7.2, *State Tax Table (Example) (Bringing Home the Gold Student Workouts)*

LESSON DESCRIPTION

Young people are sometimes surprised to learn that the pay they earn is not the same as the pay they take home. This lesson introduces students to the concepts of gross and net pay. It teaches them how to compute simple deductions, using tax tables, and to determine the take-home pay for two employees.

This lesson is correlated with national standards for economics as well as the national guidelines for personal financial management as shown in Tables 1 and 2 in the front of the book.

PARENT CONNECTION

There is no specific family activity for this lesson, but there are activities in *The Parents' Guide* that parents might want to use with this lesson. These activities are in the "Raising the Bar" section for Theme 2 in *The Parents' Guide*.

Student Objectives

At the end of this lesson the student will be able to:

✔ Identify key terms such as gross pay, net pay, deductions, and benefits.

✔ Recognize the types of benefits provided by employers.

✔ Make distinctions between required and optional deductions.

✔ Compute net pay using payroll deductions and tax tables.

The Parents' Guide is a tool for reinforcing and extending the instruction provided in the classroom. It includes:

1. Content background in the form of frequently asked questions.

2. Interesting activities that parents can do with their young adults.

3. An annotated listing of books and Internet resources related to each theme.

Workout

TIME REQUIRED **1** class period.

WARM-UP

Tell the class that the pay they earn is not the same as the pay they t___ ___e purpose of this lesson is to help the students understand the informa___ take-home pay.

EXERCISE

A. Ask the students to imagine that they have just agreed to start working a part-time job that involves working 15 hours per week at $7.00 per hour. How much will that first week's paycheck equal? (Some students might fall for your trick question and say that the first paycheck should be $105. Explain that $105 is not correct.)

B. Explain that the amount of money that appears on an employee's paycheck is not the total amount of money earned. Several deductions are taken out of paychecks. Most of these deductions are for taxes. That is how Uncle Sam takes his biggest bite.

C. Have the students read Exercise 7.1, *What Are All These Deductions from My Paycheck?* in *Student Workouts* and answer the questions. Discuss the answers.

1. What is gross pay? *(Gross pay is the total amount of money earned before any deductions are made).*

2. What is net pay? *(Net pay is the amount left after all deductions are taken out of the gross pay.)*

3. Is your paycheck the total number of hours worked times your rate of pay? *(No. Mandatory and other deductions are taken out of your paycheck.)*

4. Name three mandatory deductions. *(Federal income tax, state income tax, Social Security tax, Medicare tax, state unemployment insurance, workers' compensation insurance.)*

5. Name three other deductions. *(Life insurance, disability insurance, medical insurance, dental insurance, retirement savings plan, and contributions to charity.)*

D. Direct the students' attention to Exercise 7.2, *Calculating a Paycheck #1.* Ask the students to read the background information, the information on the form, and the information in the tax tables (Tables 7.1 and 7.2) to calculate the net pay.

E. Show Visual 7.1, *Key for Paycheck #1,* and discuss the answers with the students.

COOL DOWN

A. Direct the students' attention to Exercise 7.3, *Calculating a Paycheck #2.* Ask the students to calculate the take-home pay for Anthony McLeod. Show Visual 7.2, *Key for Paycheck #2,* and discuss their answers.

Other Training Equipment

An annotated bibliography and Internet resource list are available on our web site, **www.ncee.net**, as well as in *The Parents' Guide to Bringing Home the Gold.*

Visual 7.1

Key for Paycheck #1

Employee's Name: _____

Pay Period   ☑ Weekly   ☐ Bimonthly   ☐ Monthly

Number of allowances __1__ (0 or more)   ☑ Single   ☐ Married

GROSS PAY

1. Regular wages: _40_ Hours at _$7.00_ per hour = $280.00

2. Regular salary _____ =

                                  Gross Pay = $280.00

REQUIRED DEDUCTIONS

3. Federal Income Tax (see U.S. tax table) $27.00

4. State Income Tax (see state tax table) $10.40

5. FICA: Social Security Tax (use 6.20% x gross pay) $17.36

6. FICA: Medicare Tax (use 1.45% x gross pay) $4.06

OTHER DEDUCTIONS

7. Medical insurance   _____

8. Disability insurance   _____

9. Retirement (401k) $20.00

10. Credit union   _____

11. Union dues   _____

Total Deductions (total lines 3 through 11) $78.82

Net Pay (subtract total deductions from the gross pay) $201.18

Visual 7.2

Key for Paycheck #2

Employee's Name: _____

Pay Period   ☑ Weekly   ☐ Bimonthly   ☐ Monthly

Number of allowances ___0___ (0 or more)   ☑ Single   ☐ Married

GROSS PAY

1. Regular wages: _40_ Hours at _$9.00_ per hour =   **$360.00**

2. Regular salary _____ =   _____

               Gross Pay = _$360.00_

REQUIRED DEDUCTIONS

3. Federal Income Tax (see U.S. tax table)   _$47.00_

4. State Income Tax (see state tax table)   _$16.40_

5. FICA: Social Security Tax (use 6.20% x gross pay)   _$22.32_

6. FICA: Medicare Tax (use 1.45% x gross pay)   _$5.22_

OTHER DEDUCTIONS

7. Medical insurance   _$15.00_

8. Disability insurance   _____

9. Retirement (401k)   _$30.00_

10. Credit union   _____

11. Union dues   _____

Total Deductions (total lines 3 through 11)   _$135.94_

Net Pay (subtract total deductions from the gross pay)   _$224.06_

Financial Fitness for Life: Bringing Home the Gold Teacher Guide, ©National Council on Economic Education

THEME
3

Tomorrow's Money: Getting to the End of the Rainbow
OVERVIEW

Lesson 8

introduces the concepts of *benefit* and *opportunity cost* in spending and saving. Students participate in three activities that illustrate and reinforce the power of compound interest. Because of compounding, the benefit of early saving and investing increases in greater proportion to the opportunity cost.

Lesson 9

stresses the relationship between *risk* and *reward* in investing. Students learn about five types of investment risk and compare the risks and rewards of common types of investments.

Lesson 10

reviews the investment terms the students should have learned in the first two lessons. The students play "Investment Bingo," a vocabulary-building contest, that focuses on 24 key investment terms.

Financial Fitness for Life: Bringing Home the Gold Teacher Guide, ©National Council on Economic Education

LESSON

8

What's the Cost of Spending and Saving?

Fitness Focus

EQUIPMENT AND GETTING READY!

Make transparencies of the Visuals.

Theme 3 *Student Letter* and *Frequently Asked Questions (Bringing Home the Gold Student Workouts.)*

Visual 8.1, *The Chessboard of Financial Life*

Visual 8.2, *Save Early and Often*

Exercise 8.1, *The Opportunity Cost and Benefit of Spending and Saving (Bringing Home the Gold Student Workouts)*

Exercise 8.2, *A Tale of Two Savers (Bringing Home the Gold Student Workouts)*

Exercise 8.3, *Why It Pays to Save Early and Often (Bringing Home the Gold Student Workouts)*

Table 8.1, *The Growth of Ana's and Shawn's Savings (Bringing Home the Gold Student Workouts)*

Popcorn kernels or pennies

Family Activity 5, *The Chessboard of Financial Life (The Parents' Guide to Bringing Home the Gold)*

Family Activity 6, *Comparing Savings Plans and Places (The Parents' Guide to Bringing Home the Gold)*

LESSON DESCRIPTION

This lesson examines the benefit and opportunity cost of spending and saving. Students use a chart to learn how compound interest makes savings grow. Compounding provides an incentive to save or invest early. Because of compounding, the benefit of early saving and investing when you are young increases in greater proportion than the opportunity cost.

This lesson is correlated with national standards for economics as well as the national guidelines for personal financial management as shown in Tables 1 and 2 in the front of the book.

PARENT CONNECTION

We recommend two family activity worksheets to be used with this lesson. Family Activity Worksheet 5 in *The Parents' Guide* focuses on having students and parents play the *Chessboard of Financial Life.* This game, which was played in class, shows the power of compounding. Assign it as a reinforcement activity after the class instruction.

Family Activity Worksheet 6 in *The Parents' Guide* has students gain information about various saving plans at local financial institutions. Have the students share their findings with the class.

TIME REQUIRED

1 class period.

39

The Parents' Guide is a tool for reinforcing and extending the instruction provided in the classroom. It includes:

1. Content background in the form of frequently asked questions.

2. Interesting activities that parents can do with their young adults.

3. An annotated listing of books and Internet resources related to each theme.

Workout

WARM-UP

A. Have the students read the student letter and answer the questions that follow the letter. Discuss the answers.

Answers to the Student Letter Questions

1. Why do people save and invest? *(To increase the amount of money they have to buy goods and services later.)*

2. When is the best time to begin investing? *(Now. Because of compound interest, the earlier you start, the better.)*

3. Why do savings grow so quickly? *(The money earns compound interest, or interest on the interest.)*

4. Why do saving and investing help the overall economy? *(The money saved and invested is used to buy machines and factories for businesses. Savings are also used to help people buy homes, cars, and home improvements. Governments borrow money to build schools, highways, and parks. Without savings, the economy could not grow.)*

5. What is the relationship between investment risk and reward? *(The higher the risk, the higher the potential reward.)*

Student Objectives

At the end of this lesson the student will be able to:

✔ Identify the opportunity cost and benefit of spending and saving.

✔ Calculate investment accumulations for various interest rates and lengths of investment.

✔ Compare early and later investments and identify the benefit and opportunity cost of each strategy.

✔ Analyze and explain the impact of amount saved, time, and rate of return on savings growth.

6. What does it mean to diversify investments? *(Diversification reduces the level of risk because you have your investment "eggs" in several different baskets.)*

B. Explain to the class that this lesson focuses on deciding how much of your income you want to spend and how much of your income you want to save. Explain that spending and saving involve benefits and opportunity costs. Review with the student the definition of opportunity cost—the most valued forgone alternative of a decision.

EXERCISE

A. Have the students read Exercise 8.1, *The Opportunity Cost and Benefit of Spending and Saving* in *Students Workouts*, and answer the questions. Discuss the answers to the questions.

1. What are the benefit and the opportunity cost of spending your income today? *(The benefit is that you can immediately consume goods and services. The opportunity cost is that you have less money to use for consuming goods and services in the future.)*

2. What are the benefit and the opportunity cost of saving some of your income? *(You can enjoy consuming more goods and services later, but you will enjoy fewer goods and services today.)*

B. Have the students read Exercise 8.2, *A Tale of Two Savers,* in *Student Workouts* without examining Table 8.1, *The Growth of Ana's and Shawn's Savings,* or answering the questions. Ask the students whether Ana or Shawn will have more money at the end of his or her 65th year. You can take a show of hands or have a secret ballot. Ask some students to justify why they favor one savings plan over the other.

C. Now have the students examine Table 8.1 and answer the questions.

D. Discuss the answers to the questions.

1. How much money had Ana put into savings by age 65? *($24,000)*

2. How much money had Shawn put into savings by age 65? *($64,000)*

3. How much savings (total wealth) did Ana have at the end of her 65th year? *($993,306.59)*

4. How much savings (total wealth) did Shawn have at the end of his 65th year? *($442,503.99)*

5. In money terms, what are the opportunity cost and benefit for Ana? *(Ana sacrificed the immediate uses she might have made of $24,000, but she has $993,306.59 at age 66.)*

6. In money terms, what are the opportunity cost and benefit for Shawn? *(Shawn sacrificed the immediate uses he might have made of $64,000, but he has $442,503.09 at age 66.)*

7. What is as important as the amount saved and amount of time? Why? *(How early the money is saved and how long it is left to accumulate. These factors will determine how much wealth accumulates. Even a small amount will grow large if left to compound over a long period of time.)*

8. What are the incentives for saving early? *(Saving early means fewer contributions are necessary as compared to saving later. Compounding of interest makes money for you.)*

9. What might be an opportunity cost for saving early? *(Ana gave up buying a nicer car in order to save more.)*

10. What conclusions can you draw from this activity? *(The earlier and longer money is saved, the more money it makes. It is better to save early and put it to work than to save later and try to catch up. Although Ana saved only $24,000, her return was greater than the return for Shawn, who saved $64,000.)*

E. Ask the students why Ana had so much more money even though she saved less. Accept several reasons and write them on the board.

F. Display Visual 8.1, *The Chessboard of Financial Life.* Place a corn kernel or a penny on one of the corner squares. Ask the students if, given a choice, they would take $10,000 in cold cash OR the amount resulting from the penny or kernel in the corner doubled on the next square, and that amount doubled on the next square, and so on until each square has been used. Use corn or pennies to do the first few so they get the idea (2,4,8,16,32,64, etc.). Ask the students to explain their choices.

41

G. Next ask the students to use calculators to continue calculating the amount on the chessboard. On basic calculators, they would enter 2 x .01 = .02. Instruct them to continue hitting the = key; that will double the amount each time. Simply count as you hit the key each time. (The key sequence is sometimes reversed for scientific calculators, .01 x 2 =, or the K key must be used. Check the instructions for the calculators your students are using.) Record the amount on the transparency or board. Use corn or pennies so that students will see the visual effects of compounding. Before long, however, you will run out of space as the quantity of corn or

pennies increases. By the 21st square, students will have $10,485.76. Most basic calculators will display an error E in the upper millions in square 34. A scientific calculator will take you all the way to the end (the 64th square) and display the result in scientific notation—9.2E16, or 9 times 10 to the 16th power.

H. Tell the students that the continual process of multiplying that turned this penny or kernel into hundreds, then thousands, then millions, billions, trillions, and beyond, is called compounding. Explain that compounding is important to savers. For each dollar saved in a savings account, the bank pays interest. This interest is added to the principal, the amount originally saved; then additional interest is paid on both. This compound interest makes money grow much faster. Eventually, money will double, as pennies or corn did on this chessboard. The time it takes to double depends on the interest rate.

I. Have the students read Exercise 8.3 and answer the questions. In going over the answers, be sure to explain the *Rule of 72* and why it is important.

Answers to Exercise 8.3

Investment	Interest or rate of return	Years to double
Passbook savings	3%	24 years
Money market account	6%	12 years
U.S. Treasury Bond	7%	10.2 years
Stock market	12%	6 years

1. One key point in the economic way of thinking is that people respond to incentives. What is the incentive for saving early and often? *(The benefit of substantial wealth accumulation over time.)*

COOL DOWN

A. Display Visual 8.2, *Save Early and Often*, and explain the factors that influence how much wealth a person can accumulate.

1. Point out the opportunity costs of and incentives for saving and investing, and review the factors that determine the amount that will be accumulated.

2. Divide the students into small groups.

3. Explain that each group is responsible for developing a 30-second radio advertisement that explains the relationship among amount saved, interest rate, and time. The ad should be targeted at high school students and young adults.

4. Give the groups time to prepare their ads.

5. Have each group present its ad to the class.

6. Evaluate the ads using these criteria:

- How well they explained how time affects the growth of savings.

- How well they explained how the amount of money deposited affects the growth of savings.

- How well they explained how the rate of interest affects the growth of savings.

- How effective is the creativity and appeal of the ad.

Other Training Equipment

An annotated bibliography and Internet resource list are available on our web site, **www.ncee.net**, as well as in *The Parents' Guide to Bringing Home the Gold.*

Visual 8.1

The Chessboard of Financial Life

Visual 8.2

Save Early and Often

The factors that affect
how much savings grow are:

Time

The earlier or longer you save,
the more savings you will have.

Investment Size

The more you save each year
from your income,
the more savings you will have.

Rate of Return

The higher the interest rate
or rate of return, the more savings
you will have.

LESSON

9

There Is No Free Lunch in Investing

Fitness Focus

EQUIPMENT AND GETTING READY!

Make transparencies of the Visuals.

✔ Visual 9.1, *There Is No Free Lunch in Investing*

✔ Visual 9.2, *The Pyramid of Risk and Reward*

✔ Exercise 9.1, *Types of Investment Risk (Bringing Home the Gold Student Workouts)*

✔ Exercise 9.2, *The Pyramid of Risk and Reward (Bringing Home the Gold Student Workouts)*

✔ Family Activity 7, *Be an Investment Guru (The Parents' Guide to Bringing Home the Gold)*

LESSON DESCRIPTION

Risk is inherent in all investments. In investing, there are risks you cannot control. However, other risks can be controlled. The key is to develop a risk-reward ratio with which you are comfortable.

The higher the risk, the greater the potential reward. This is why there is no free lunch in investing. In this lesson, students learn about five types of risk and then compare the risks and rewards of several of the most frequently used investment vehicles. The lesson provides an overview of the investment world.

This lesson is correlated with national standards for economics as well as the national guidelines for personal financial management as shown in Tables 1 and 2 in the front of the book.

PARENT CONNECTION

Family Activity Worksheet 6 in *The Parents' Guide* focuses on having each family member select a stock and follow it for a period of time. You might want students to report periodically on the outcomes of using this activity in their families.

The Parents' Guide is a tool for reinforcing and extending the instruction provided in the classroom. It includes:

1. Content background in the form of frequently asked questions.

2. Interesting activities that parents can do with their young adults.

3. An annotated listing of books and Internet resources related to each theme.

46

Workout

WARM-UP

Explain to the students that they have learned that investing pays off in the long run. However, all investments are not created equal.

EXERCISE

A. Display Visual 9.1, *There Is No Free Lunch in Investing*. Explain the relationship between risk and reward.

B. Have the students read Exercise 9.1, *Types of Investment Risk* in *Student Workouts*. Then discuss the risks.

C. Have the students answer the questions in Exercise 9.1. Discuss the answers to the questions.

1. **What is the annual rate of return on an investment?** *(The extra money you receive in a year on your investment divided by the amount of the original investment stated on a yearly basis.)*

2. **If you earn $40 a year on a $500 investment, what is the annual rate of return?** *(8% [$40 ÷ $500 = .08 or 8%])*

3. **What is the relationship between the expected rate of return and the investment risk?** *(The greater the investment risk, the greater the expected rate of return.)*

4. **If the annual nominal rate of return on an investment is 10% and the annual rate of inflation is 3%, what is the real rate of return?** *(7% [10% - 3% = 7%])*

5. **True, false, or uncertain and why? "The Internet is the future of our economy. The prices of Internet stocks are bound to go up."** *(Uncertain or false. Investors could change their attitudes toward Internet stocks.)*

TIME REQUIRED

2 class periods.

Student Objectives

At the end of this lesson the student will be able to:

✔ Describe five types of investment risk.

✔ Describe the relationship between investment risk and investment reward.

✔ Distinguish between real and nominal rates of return.

✔ Describe the characteristics of several investments, including savings accounts, stocks, bonds, mutual funds, and real estate.

✔ Analyze the pyramid of risk and reward.

✔ Compare and contrast the risks and rewards of several types of investments.

6. **True, false, or uncertain and why? "This investment pays 30% a year and is perfectly safe. I put my mother's money into this investment."** *(False. Investments with high potential rates of return always involve risk.)*

D. Project Visual 9.2, *The Pyramid of Risk and Reward*. Discuss why investments are placed where they are on the pyramid of risk and reward.

E. Divide the class into groups of three. Have the groups rate the risk and the reward of each type of investment in the exercise.

F. Discuss each type of investment. When groups differ, ask them to explain the reasons for their rankings. The answers provided are not cast in stone. The key is that the students understand the risk-reward ratio.

47

Mattress

Financial Risk	1	2	**3**
Market Price Risk	**1**	2	3
Liquidity Risk	**1**	2	3
Inflation Risk	1	2	**3**
Reward	**1**	2	3

Why? The money could be stolen. You can get it any time you want, but you don't earn a rate of return. If there is inflation, your real rate of return will be negative.

Regular (Passbook) Savings Account

Financial Risk	**1**	2	3
Market Price Risk	**1**	2	3
Liquidity Risk	**1**	2	3
Inflation Risk	1	**2**	3
Reward	**1**	2	3

Why? You will not lose your money, but the interest rates are low. Liquidity is high; you can get your money out at any time.

Certificate of Deposit

Financial Risk	**1**	2	3
Market Price Risk	**1**	2	3
Liquidity Risk	1	**2**	3
Inflation Risk	1	**2**	3
Reward	1	**2**	3

Why? Insured accounts involve little risk. Banks usually pay a higher rate of interest if you keep your money in longer. Deposits can be withdrawn at any time, but there is a penalty for withdrawal before maturity date.

U.S. Government Savings Bonds

Financial Risk	**1**	2	3
Market Price Risk	**1**	2	3
Liquidity Risk	1	**2**	3
Inflation Risk	1	**2**	3
Reward	1	**2**	3

Why? The government prints money, so these bonds are safe. There is some risk that you will lock in a lower interest rate than what the market pays as you hold the bond. You can receive your money anytime, although there could be a penalty if it is withdrawn before maturity. In recent years, rates have been higher than for passbook savings accounts.

Money Market Mutual Funds

Financial Risk	1	**2**	3
Market Price Risk	**1**	2	3
Liquidity Risk	**1**	2	3
Inflation Risk	**1**	2	3
Reward	1	**2**	3

Why? They are safe but not insured. Earnings are sometimes higher than with savings accounts. You can get your money anytime.

Stocks

Financial Risk	1	**2**	3
Market Price Risk	1	2	**3**
Liquidity Risk	1	**2**	3
Inflation Risk	1	**2**	3
Reward	1	2	**3**

Why? Stocks have high potential rewards and high inflation, financial, and market risks. Also, some stocks are sold fraudulently. The market price risk depends on how speculative the stock is.

Stock Mutual Funds

Financial Risk	1	**2**	3
Market Price Risk	1	**2**	3
Liquidity Risk	**1**	2	3
Inflation Risk	1	**2**	3
Reward	1	2	**3**

Why? Stock mutual funds have the risks of stocks but offer more diversity. They can be bought and sold daily and so have liquidity.

Real Estate

Financial Risk	1	**2**	3
Market Price Risk	1	**2**	3
Liquidity Risk	1	2	**3**
Inflation Risk	1	**2**	3
Reward	1	**2**	3

Why? Real estate prices depend on supply and demand in the neighborhood where the property is located. Prices can change if the neighborhood becomes more or less desirable. Also, it is not always easy to sell real estate, particularly if mortgage rates are high.

COOL DOWN

The Savings Game

A. Tell the students that they have $5,000 to invest, and they must choose the best investment.

B. Write each investment on a sheet of paper. You can use different colors for different investments if you wish. The investments are:

- Mattress
- Passbook savings account
- Certificate of deposit
- U.S. Government Savings Bond
- Money market mutual fund
- Stocks
- Stock mutual fund

NOTE: Don't use real estate; there are non-investment reasons to buy a house.

C. Put the sheets of paper on different parts of your classroom floor.

D. Ask the students to stand near the paper of the investment they would choose.

E. Ask each student to defend his or her investment in terms of risk and reward. First, this will indicate whether the student understands the concept. More importantly, their answers will illustrate that investors view the risk-reward ratio differently. Investors must know themselves and be comfortable with the risks they take.

Other Training Equipment

An annotated bibliography and Internet resource list are available on our web site, **www.ncee.net**, as well as in *The Parents' Guide to Bringing Home the Gold.*

49

Visual 9.1

There Is No Free Lunch in Investing

Investment return is the
additional income earned
from saving or investing money.

Risk is the uncertainty that you will
receive the expected return.

The greater the risk,
the higher the expected return.

Investors are paid to take risks.
There is no free lunch in investing.

Visual 9.2

The Pyramid of Risk and Reward

**Highest Risk/
Highest Potential Return or Loss**

Speculative Stocks

Real Estate

Individual Stocks

Stock Mutual Funds

Money Market Mutual Funds

Insured Certificates of Deposit

Insured Savings Accounts

U.S. Savings Bond

U.S. Government Securities

**Lowest Risk/
Lowest Potential Return or Loss**

Financial Fitness for Life: Bringing Home the Gold Teacher Guide, ©National Council on Economic Education

LESSON

10

Investment Bingo

Fitness Focus

EQUIPMENT
AND GETTING READY!

More than usual pre-class preparation is required for this lesson. A sufficient number of markers (Activity 10A) must be made so there are 24 markers for each student. The definitions and terms in Activity 10B should each be put on a separate card or paper.

Make a transparency of the Visual.

✔ Visual 10.1, *Investment Bingo*

✔ Exercise 10.1, *Investment Bingo (Bringing Home the Gold Student Workouts)*

✔ Activity 10A, *Investment Bingo Markers*

✔ Activity 10B, *Investment Bingo Balls*

✔ Box for "Bingo" slips

LESSON DESCRIPTION

Knowledgeable investing involves choosing among many alternatives. A first step is to learn the language of investing and to understand at least some of the basic investment alternatives. *Investment Bingo* is a vocabulary-building contest involving investment terms. By playing bingo, the students learn the definitions of 24 key investment terms studied in the previous two lessons.

This lesson is correlated with national standards for economics as well as the national guidelines for personal financial management as shown in Tables 1 and 2 in the front of this book.

PARENT CONNECTION

There is no specific family activity for this lesson, but there are activities in *The Parents' Guide* that parents might want to use with this lesson. These activities can be found in the "Raising the Bar" section for Theme 3.

The Parents' Guide is a tool for reinforcing and extending the instruction provided in the classroom. It includes:

1. Content background in the form of frequently asked questions.
2. Interesting activities that parents can do with their young adults.
3. An annotated listing of books and Internet resources related to each theme.

Student Objectives

At the end of this lesson the student will be able to:

✔ Define key investment terms.

✔ Define the characteristics of investment alternatives.

Workout

WARM-UP

Tell the students that they will play *Investment Bingo* to see how well they learned the terms in Lessons 8 and 9.

EXERCISE

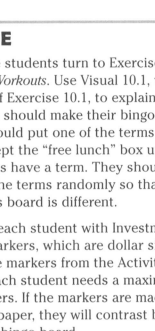

A. Have the students turn to Exercise 10.1 in *Student Workouts*. Use Visual 10.1, which is a copy of Exercise 10.1, to explain how the students should make their bingo boards. They should put one of the terms in each box except the "free lunch" box until all of the boxes have a term. They should distribute the terms randomly so that each student's board is different.

B. Provide each student with Investment Bingo markers, which are dollar signs. Make the markers from the Activity 10A sheet. Each student needs a maximum of 24 markers. If the markers are made from colored paper, they will contrast better with the bingo board.

C. Cut up the Investment Bingo slips of paper from Activity 10B. Place the slips of paper in a box.

D. Draw the bingo balls (slips of paper) out of the box one at a time. When a definition is read, each student should place a bingo marker on the correct term. If they don't know the term that fits the definition, they are out of luck.

E. Students should yell "Bingo!" whenever they have five markers in a line horizontally, vertically, or diagonally. All students get a bingo marker on the "free lunch" square. Check the correctness of their placement.

F. After each game, mix the slips of paper and play another round until the students are familiar with the definitions.

COOL DOWN

Have the students write the definition of each term at the bottom of their bingo board. An alternative would be to read the term and call on a student to define each term.

Other Training Equipment

An annotated bibliography and Internet resource list are available on our web site, **www.ncee.net**, as well as in *The Parents' Guide to Bringing Home the Gold*.

Visual 10.1

Investment Bingo

		Free Lunch		

Investment
Bingo Markers

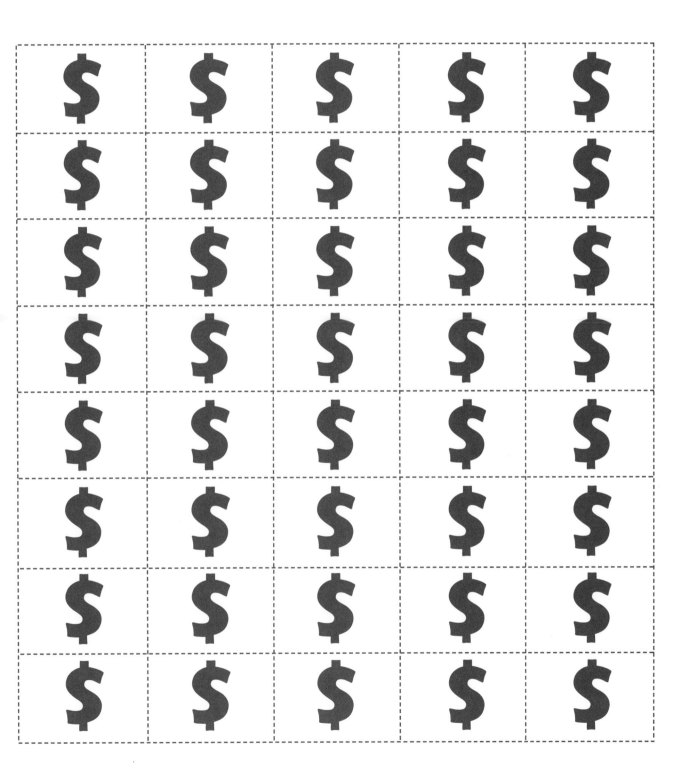

Investment Bingo Balls

Instructions: Each bingo ball is actually a slip of paper. Cut each definition and answer along the dotted line to make strips. You could put the definitions on cards and laminate them so they can be used again.

THE INCOME EARNED FROM AN INVESTMENT DIVIDED BY THE AMOUNT OF THE INVESTMENT
Rate of return

INTEREST THAT IS NOT ONLY EARNED ON THE PRINCIPAL BUT ALSO ON THE INTEREST ALREADY EARNED
Compound interest

WHAT YOU GIVE UP IN ORDER TO GET SOMETHING ELSE—THE NEXT BEST ALTERNATIVE
Opportunity cost

A REWARD THAT INFLUENCES CHOICES
Incentive

THE MONEY A PERSON EARNS DURING A PARTICULAR TIME PERIOD, OFTEN ONE YEAR
Income

THE AMOUNT OF MONEY A PERSON ACCUMULATES, OR TOTAL ASSETS MINUS TOTAL LIABILITIES
Wealth/Net Worth

A RULE FOR DETERMINING HOW LONG IT TAKES MONEY TO DOUBLE AT A PARTICULAR RATE OF RETURN
Rule of 72

THE RISK THAT A BUSINESS OR GOVERNMENT WILL NOT BE ABLE TO RETURN YOUR MONEY
Financial risk

THE RISK THAT THE PRICE OF AN INVESTMENT WILL GO DOWN BECAUSE OF SUPPLY AND DEMAND
Market price risk

THE RISK THAT AN INVESTMENT WILL BE DIFFICULT TO TURN INTO CASH
Liquidity risk

THE RATE OF RETURN FROM AN INVESTMENT AFTER ADJUSTING FOR INFLATION
Real rate of return

THE RISK THAT AN INVESTMENT HAS BEEN MISREPRESENTED
Fraud risk

THE RATE OF RETURN FROM AN INVESTMENT BEFORE ADJUSTING FOR INFLATION
Nominal rate of return

A FEDERALLY INSURED ACCOUNT AT A BANK, SAVINGS AND LOAN, OR CREDIT UNION FROM WHICH YOU CAN WITHDRAW YOUR MONEY AT ANY TIME
Passbook savings account

A TYPE OF SAVINGS DEPOSIT THAT YOU MUST LEAVE IN A BANK FOR A SPECIFIED PERIOD OF TIME
Certificate of deposit

A U.S. GOVERNMENT BOND THAT YOU CAN INVEST IN FOR AS LITTLE AS $50
U.S. Savings Bond

THE ADDITIONAL MONEY EARNED ON AN INVESTMENT IN PERCENTAGE TERMS FOR A YEAR
Annual rate of return

A GENERAL RISE IN THE PRICE LEVEL
Inflation

A MUTUAL FUND THAT INCLUDES LOANS TO BUSINESSES AND GOVERNMENTS FOR SHORT PERIODS OF TIME
Money market mutual fund

SHARES OF OWNERSHIP IN A CORPORATION
Stocks

A MUTUAL FUND THAT HAS MORE RISKS AND MORE POTENTIAL REWARDS
Stock mutual fund

BUYING A HOME IS AN EXAMPLE OF THIS TYPE OF INVESTMENT
Real estate

THE RISK THAT THE REAL VALUE OF YOUR INVESTMENT WILL DECREASE BECAUSE OF A RISE IN THE PRICE LEVEL
Inflation risk

THE GREATER THE RISK, THE GREATER THE POTENTIAL REWARD
Risk/Reward ratio

57

THEME

4

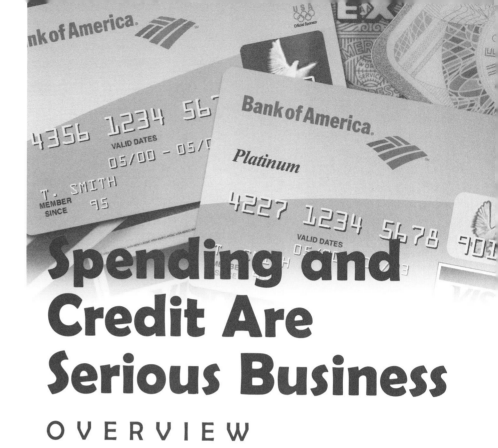

Spending and Credit Are Serious Business

OVERVIEW

This fourth theme introduces students to the wise use of credit and credit protection.

Lesson 11

provides an overview of what *credit* is and some of the advantages and disadvantages of using credit. Students examine various types of loans including home mortgages, car loans, college loans, personal loans, and credit card loans.

Lesson 12

asks the students to act as *financial advisors*. They provide advice to their "clients" on when it may or may not be appropriate to use different forms of credit.

Lesson 13

explains what a *credit report* is and how to read one. The students then play the role of loan officers and review excerpts from the credit report of loan applicants. They evaluate each applicant's credit history and use the information to determine whether to grant the loan request.

Lesson 14

teaches students how to compute *finance charges*, how to differentiate between add-on and annual percentage rates, and how the annual percentage rate and loan repayment period affect the cost of a loan.

Lesson 15

emphasizes that *credit cards* differ in terms of the annual fee, annual percentage rate, grace period, and credit limit. Students learn to read a credit card statement so they can see the real cost of charging goods and services.

Lesson 16

introduces how to use a computer loan calculator to determine the *cost of a loan*. This technique is particularly important for mortgage calculation. There are many loan calculators on the Internet, and many software packages, such as *Quicken,* also contain loan calculators.

Lesson 17

stresses the skills students need to *shop for credit* by filling out a credit comparison chart for a hypothetical loan. Using the same techniques, the students then shop online for a loan. Finally, the students compare the cost of the same loan at various local lending institutions.

Lesson 18

provides an overview of *consumer credit protection*. It stresses the federal laws designed to protect credit consumers from lenders' mistakes. These include the Truth in Lending Act, Fair Credit Reporting Act, Equal Credit Opportunity Act, Fair Credit Billing Act, Fair Debt Collection Practices Act, and, most recently, the Electronic Fund Transfer Act.

Lesson 19

reminds students that while most credit transactions are completely legal, there are some that are not. This lesson introduces *scams and schemes* such as identify theft, loan scams, and credit repair loans. The lesson also features legal but high-cost credit practices prevalent in urban areas such as payday loans and rent-to-own plans.

LESSON

11

What Is Credit?

Fitness Focus

EQUIPMENT AND GETTING READY!

✔ Theme 4 *Student Letter* and *Frequently Asked Questions* (Bringing Home the Gold Student Workouts)

✔ Exercise 11.1, *What Is Credit?* (Bringing Home the Gold Student Workouts)

✔ Exercise 11.2, *Common Forms of Credit* (Bringing Home the Gold Student Workouts)

✔ Exercise 11.3, *Credit Research* (Bringing Home the Gold Student Workouts)

LESSON DESCRIPTION

Credit decisions are among the most important choices that young people will make. This lesson provides an overview of what credit is and some of the advantages and disadvantages of using credit. Students examine various types of loans including home mortgages, car loans, college loans, personal loans, and credit card loans.

This lesson is correlated with national standards for economics as well as the national guidelines for personal financial management as shown in Tables 1 and 2 in the front of this book.

PARENT CONNECTION

There is no specific family activity for this lesson, but there are activities in *The Parents' Guide* that parents might want to use with this lesson. These activities can be found in the "Raising the Bar" section for Theme 4.

The Parents' Guide is a tool for reinforcing and extending the instruction provided in the classroom. It includes:

1. Content background in the form of frequently asked questions.

2. Interesting activities that parents can do with their young adults.

3. An annotated listing of books and Internet resources related to each theme.

TIME REQUIRED

1 class period.

60

Workout

WARM-UP

A. Have the students read the *Student Letter* in *Student Workouts* and answer the questions at the end of letter.

Answers to the Student Letter Questions

1. What is credit? *(Credit means obtaining the use of money that you do not have. Obtaining credit means convincing an individual or a financial institution to voluntarily provide a loan to you in return for a promise to pay it back later, generally with an additional charge called interest.)*

2. What is an advantage to using credit? *(Using credit allows you to use a good or a service today and pay for it later. Using credit can help people acquire valuable assets and can add to the enjoyment of life.)*

3. What is a disadvantage to using credit? *(Loans have to be repaid. Lenders charge interest for the use of their money. Individuals have to sacrifice things they wish to have today because they are required to pay for goods or services they have already consumed.)*

4. What do lenders look for when they approve a loan to an individual? *(Character, capacity, and collateral.)*

5. Do credit consumers have legal protection? *(Several state and federal laws are designed to protect credit consumers from dishonest business practices.)*

Student Objectives

At the end of this lesson the student will be able to:

✔ Identify key terms such as credit, interest, and risk.

✔ Recognize the advantages and disadvantages of using credit.

✔ Identify types of financial institutions.

✔ Explain that most credit transactions are voluntary ones in which both sides gain.

B. Explain that this lesson will introduce students to credit. Students will learn about when the advantages of using credit outweigh the disadvantages. Stress the idea that decisions regarding the use of credit are similar to other choices. There are advantages and disadvantages to using credit.

EXERCISE

A. Have the students read Exercise 11.1, *What Is Credit?* in *Student Workouts*. Ask the students to answer the questions. Discuss the answers.

1. What is credit? *(Credit allows individuals to obtain the use of money that they do not have. In return, people who use credit repay the amount they borrow, plus interest.)*

2. What is the bright side of using credit? *(Credit can help people in many ways— by enabling them to acquire valuable assets, by helping out with emergency expenses.)*

3. What is the dark side of using credit?
(People sometimes use too much credit in relationship to their income. As a result these people spend a lot of their current income on previous purchases, leaving them with less money to buy things they may currently want.)

4. What institutions are sources of credit?
(Commercial banks, savings and loans, credit unions, and consumer finance companies.)

5. What is interest? *(Interest is the compensation that owners of financial institutions expect to receive when they make loans.)*

6. Who most often wins in a credit transaction? *(Ordinarily, both parties are better off as a result of a credit transaction.)*

7. How does risk influence the rate of interest? *(Higher-risk loans usually result in higher interest rates. Lower-risk loans result in lower interest rates.)*

8. What is collateral? *(Collateral is an asset used to back a loan.)*

B. Direct the students' attention to Exercise 11.2, *Common Forms of Credit*. Explain the types of lenders listed.

1. Commercial banks and savings and loans are very similar in the types of financial services they provide their customers; these include loans, savings accounts, and checking accounts.

2. Commercial banks and savings and loans are regulated by different agencies.

3. Credit unions are not-for-profit cooperatives—enterprises owned by their members—that provide many of the same financial services as commercial banks and savings and loans.

4. Consumer finance companies lend money to individuals usually for things such as automobiles or household appliances. Often their customers do not qualify for bank credit and therefore pay a higher rate of interest.

C. Ask the students to read the additional information provided in the chart in Exercise 11.2, *Common Forms of Credit*, and answer the questions. Discuss the answers.

1. What are the advantages of home loans and college loans compared to credit card and personal loans? *(Home and college loans usually help people acquire assets that increase in value. Interest rates on these loans are usually lower than for credit cards or personal loans.)*

2. What are the disadvantages of credit card and college loans? *(Sometimes young people borrow more than they should for college loans and overuse credit card loans.)*

D. Review some of the key points in this lesson. Ask:

1. What is a key advantage of using credit? *(Using credit allows you to use a good or a service today and pay for it later. Using credit can help people acquire valuable assets—like a college education or a home. Credit can also add to the enjoyment of life.)*

2. What is a key disadvantage of using credit? *(When credit is easily available, some people spend more than they otherwise would. Loans have to be repaid. Lenders charge interest for the use of their money. Individuals who borrow heavily have to sacrifice things they wish to have today because they are required to pay for goods or services they have already consumed.)*

3. Who gains from credit transactions? *(Almost always, both sides in a credit transaction benefit. Borrowers are able to purchase something that may be of value today and perhaps in the future. Lenders are repaid the money that they loaned, plus interest.)*

Financial Fitness for Life: Bringing Home the Gold Teacher Guide, ©National Council on Economic Education

COOL DOWN

Direct the students' attention to Exercise 11.3, *Credit Research*. Ask the students to contact local financial institutions to determine the annual percentage rate for the various types of personal loans listed in the chart. You may wish to have the students discuss this information with the other members of the class.

Other Training Equipment

An annotated bibliography and Internet resource list are available on our web site, **www.ncee.net**, as well as in *The Parents' Guide to Bringing Home the Gold.*

63

LESSON

12

Making Credit Choices

Fitness Focus

EQUIPMENT

✔ Exercise 12.1, *Fickle Financial Advisors (Bringing Home the Gold Student Workouts)*

TIME REQUIRED
1 class period.

LESSON DESCRIPTION

Individuals face many credit choices. Students in this lesson act as financial advisors providing advice on when it may or may not be appropriate to use different forms of credit.

This lesson is correlated with national standards for economics as well as the national guidelines for personal financial management as shown in Tables 1 and 2 in the front of this book.

PARENT CONNECTION

There is no specific family activity for this lesson, but there are activities in *The Parents' Guide* that parents might want to use with this lesson. These activities can be found in the "Raising the Bar" section for Theme 4.

The Parents' Guide is a tool for reinforcing and extending the instruction provided in the classroom. It includes:

1. Content background in the form of frequently asked questions.
2. Interesting activities that parents can do with their young adults.
3. An annotated listing of books and Internet resources related to each theme.

Student Objectives

At the end of this lesson the student will be able to:

✔ Identify advantages and disadvantages of using credit.

✔ Make decisions about the wise use of credit.

Workout

WARM-UP

Explain that the purpose of this lesson is to help the students practice making wise decisions regarding the use of credit. The students will gain practice in identifying when the advantages of using credit outweigh the disadvantages.

EXERCISE

A. Explain that the students are going to play the role of financial advisors. Direct the students' attention to Exercise 12.1, *Fickle Financial Advisors* in *Student Workouts.* Have the students read *Part 1: Your Job.*

B. Divide the class into small groups. Ask the students in each group to read the four situations in *Part 2: Four Clients.* The groups should decide on the advantages of using credit, the disadvantages of using credit, and make a recommendation to each of their four clients.

C. After the students have read and discussed the cases of the clients, discuss their recommendations with the whole class. Here are the suggested answers.

Client 1

1. **What is the main advantage of getting credit?** *(The credit will be used to purchase a college education, which is a valuable asset. This education is an asset that will provide the client with an income as a chemical engineer beginning in four years.)*

2. **What is the main disadvantage of getting credit?** *(The college loan is for a relatively large amount of money.)*

3. **Do you recommend that this client apply for the loan?** *(Yes. The college education sought by Client 1 will enable her to earn more over several years of working than the amount of credit being sought.)*

Client 2

1. **What is the main advantage of getting credit?** *(The television set will add enjoyment to life today.)*

2. **What is main disadvantage of getting credit?** *(A television set is not a valuable asset since it loses value very quickly. Also, in a short period of time, Client 2 will be earning a living and moving to an apartment; the move may involve many unexpected expenses.)*

3. **Do you recommend that this client apply for the loan?** *(No. The television set sought by Client 2 will not maintain its value. Client 2 could buy a less expensive television set now, or wait to purchase a television after the move to the apartment.)*

Client 3

1. **What is the main advantage of getting credit?** *(Fun with school friends before graduation.)*

2. **What is main disadvantage of getting credit?** *(A vacation does not retain much value. Once a vacation is consumed, all that is left are the memories. Using the credit card is an expensive way to pay for a vacation. It seems likely that Client 3 will not be able to pay the bill right away and so will pay a great deal of interest.)*

3. **Do you recommend that this client apply for the loan?** *(No. The vacation sought by Client 3 will not retain much value. It will be expensive in terms of credit card interest. In a short time, Client 3 will finish college and get a job. We suspect that in the relatively near future, Client 3 will be much better able to afford a vacation.)*

Client 4

Client 4

1. **What is the main advantage of getting credit**? *(Obtaining a car loan will help Client 4 arrive safely and promptly at work each day.)*

2. **What is main disadvantage of getting credit?** *(Car loans can be burdensome and new cars lose their value quickly.)*

3. **Do you recommend that this client apply for the loan?** *(We think Client 4 would be wise to obtain the car loan and buy the car. It is a good investment in the client's future earnings, and the new car will be a lot safer than driving the car the client now has.)*

D. Review some of the key points in this lesson. Ask:

- **What is a key advantage of using credit?** *(Using credit allows you to obtain a good or a service today and pay for it later.*

Using credit can help people acquire assets that retain or increase in value—like a college education or a home. Credit can also add to the enjoyment of life and help in an emergency.)

- **What is a key disadvantage of using credit?** *(When credit is easily available, some people spend more than they otherwise would. Loans have to be repaid. Lenders charge interest for the use of their money. Individuals have to sacrifice things they wish to have today because they are required to pay for goods or services they have already consumed.)*

- **Who gains from credit transactions?** *(Usually, both sides in a credit transaction benefit. Borrowers are able to purchase something that may be of value today and perhaps in the future. Lenders are repaid the money they loaned, plus interest.)*

COOL DOWN

Ask the class to again act as Fickle Financial Advisors. Read this case to the students and ask them to state the advantages and disadvantages of seeking credit and their recommendation.

We are a newly married couple. Both of us are 28 years old. We have a fashionable apartment with great furniture. The deck from our apartment overlooks a sumptuous swimming pool and the tennis courts. We have good jobs and good incomes. We are regarded as upwardly mobile professionals. In our professions, you are what you drive. Currently, we drive a stodgy, late model car that has 75,000 miles on it. We want to look the part of prosperous young professionals. We are thinking about buying a very nice luxury car with all the coolest features. We work hard. We deserve it. We will need to borrow about $35,000. That may sound like a lot but you haven't seen this car! Besides, the car dealer says we can afford the monthly payments.

1. **What is the main advantage of getting credit?** *(Driving a great car and feeling prosperous.)*

2. **What is main disadvantage of getting credit?** *(The car payments will mean that the clients must give up other things they might want. Cars are assets that lose their value quickly.)*

3. **Do you recommend that these clients apply for the loan?** *(No. The car is an asset that will lose its value quickly and it involves a large financial sacrifice for this couple. Here is our suggestion. Drive the old car a while longer. Save the money that would have gone into the car payment and put it toward a down payment on a new house. Houses usually increase in value while cars usually do not. These clients will probably be more prosperous as owners of a new house rather than a new luxury car. We know that while we are no fun at all, we give good financial advice.)*

Other Training Equipment

An annotated bibliography and Internet resource list are available on our web site, **www.ncee.net**, as well as in *The Parents' Guide to Bringing Home the Gold*.

LESSON

13

Applying for Credit

Fitness Focus

EQUIPMENT
AND GETTING READY!

✔ Exercise 13.1, *Reading a Credit Report (Bringing Home the Gold Student Workouts)*

✔ Exercise 13.2, *Evaluating a Credit Report (Bringing Home the Gold Student Workouts)*

✔ Exercise 13.3, *Evaluating Three Loan Applications (Bringing Home the Gold Student Workouts)*

✔ Illustration 13.1, *Credit Report of John Q. Consumer (Bringing Home the Gold Student Workouts)*

LESSON DESCRIPTION

This lesson explains what a credit report is and how to read one. The students play the role of loan officers and review excerpts from the credit reports of loan applicants. They evaluate each applicant's credit history and use the information to determine whether to grant the loan request.

This lesson is correlated with national standards for economics as well as the national guidelines for personal financial management as shown in Tables 1 and 2 in the front of this book.

PARENT CONNECTION

There is no specific family activity for this lesson, but there are activities in *The Parents' Guide* that parents can use with this lesson. These activities can be found in the "Raising the Bar" section for Theme 4.

The Parents' Guide is a tool for reinforcing and extending the instruction provided in the classroom. It includes:

TIME REQUIRED
1 and one-half class periods.

1. Content background in the form of frequently asked questions.

2. Interesting activities that parents can do with their young adults.

3. An annotated listing of books and Internet resources related to each theme.

Workout

WARM-UP

Ask the students to describe the job of a loan officer at a bank or savings and loan. Have they ever wondered what goes through these people's minds when considering loan applications? Today the students will have a chance to find out. They will learn about the principal tool used by loan officers—the credit report—by studying a sample. They will then assume the role of loan officer, review excerpts from the credit reports of three loan applicants, and make a decision about whether to approve the loans.

EXERCISE

A. Ask your students to imagine that an individual has approached them and asked to borrow a substantial sum of money. What would they want to know about this person before they decided to lend the money? List responses on the board.

B. Have the students read Exercise 13.1, *Reading a Credit Report.* After the students have read it, ask:

1. **What are the "3 Cs of Credit"?** *(Character, capacity, collateral.)*

2. **Give examples of each of the 3 Cs of Credit.** *(Answers will vary.)*

3. **What is a credit report?** *(A record of an individual's credit history.)*

4. **Why should a person care about his or her credit report?** *(A good credit rating is important if a person wants to borrow money—particularly at a competitive interest rate.)*

5. **Are you allowed to check the accuracy of your credit report?** *(Yes. The Fair Credit Reporting Act gives you this right.)*

6. **Is there a charge for checking the accuracy of your credit report?** *(There is no charge if you have been turned down for a loan. There is a charge, however, if you just want to check it.)*

Student Objectives

At the end of this lesson the student will be able to:

✔ Identify the qualities that a lender looks for in a loan applicant.

✔ Describe what a credit report is and how it is used.

✔ List the types of information contained in a credit report.

✔ Compare and contrast favorable and unfavorable credit reports.

✔ Use a credit report to determine whether to grant a loan.

C. Have the students complete Exercise 13.2 using Illustration 13.1. Discuss the answers to the questions.

1. **Whose credit report is this?** *(John Q. Consumer.)*

2. **How many potentially negative items are listed?** *(Four. Two are from public records and two from accounts with creditors and others.)*

3. **How many accounts are in good standing?** *(Three.)*

4. **On page 2, there are two very negative items. What are they?**

   a. *(Dime Saving filed a civil claim against John Q. Consumer.)*

   b. *(John Q. Consumer filed for bankruptcy, and it was discharged, or granted.)*

5. Have any of John Q. Consumer's credit cards been lost or stolen? *(Yes. The card issued by America Finance Corporation.)*

6. Does John Q. Consumer have a good credit record with First Credit Union and National Credit Card? What are the reasons for your opinion? *(Yes. The status is open—never late.)*

7. Who requested John Q. Consumer's credit report in 1999?

a. *Credit R Us*

b. *World Bank*

c. *Fidelity Bank NA*

8. Is John Q. Consumer a homeowner? *(Yes.)*

9. What is the most negative item on this report, and for how many years does that item stay on the credit report? *(The bankruptcy. It is in the report until 11/07 or ten years after the bankruptcy was discharged.)*

10. If you were a lender, would you grant John Q. Consumer credit? Why or why not? *(Answers will vary.)*

D. Invite the students to play the role of a loan officer and read Exercise 13.3, *Evaluating Three Loan Applications* in *Student Workouts*. This page presents credit report summaries for each of three individuals applying for credit. Students will play the role of the loan officer and check a box that either grants or denies the credit request based on the information presented.

E. Ask the students to review the three credit report summaries and make their decisions. An alternative activity is to have the students work in groups. Have each group make a decision on each applicant. **Important! Reinforce the concept that in a real lending decision, the loan officer, or creditor, would require a completed loan application, and the decision would be made on more information than just a credit report. For this exercise, we will assume that the applicant meets all other qualifications.**

F. Ask the students for their decisions and the reasoning behind them. Here are some answers.

- **Janice Brown.** She should be declined. She has shown a chronic inability to pay her bills on time.

- **Tito Sanders.** He should be approved. He has an excellent credit record and has always paid his bills in the manner agreed upon.

- **Maria Martinez.** She is a candidate for the "not sure" category. Approvals and denials seem equally appropriate. Although she has had some problems in the past, her recent record is good. Possibly she had medical bills in the early to mid-1990s, and these are reflected in the "past due" category. Suggest that the students may want to give her the benefit of the doubt and have further discussions with her, trying to understand what caused her financial problems in the past and what was done to resolve them.

COOL DOWN

Put the students in groups and have each group draw up a list of steps that can be taken to establish or re-establish a good credit rating. Have each group report to the class. Some steps are:

- Pay bills on time.
- Borrow only what you need.
- Apply for and use only a few credit cards.
- Open a savings account and make deposits monthly.
- Open a checking account and don't bounce checks.

- Report a lost or stolen credit card immediately.
- Use collateral to strengthen loan requests.
- Avoid bankruptcy.
- Stay employed.
- Own a home and don't move too often.
- Make sure your loans aren't too great a percentage of your income.

Other Training Equipment

An annotated bibliography and Internet resource list are available on our web site, **www.ncee.net**, as well as in *The Parents' Guide to Bringing Home the Gold.*

LESSON

14

All About Interest

Fitness Focus

EQUIPMENT AND GETTING READY!

Make a transparency of the Visual.

✔ Visual 14.1, *Interest Rate Problems*

✔ Exercise 14.1, *Everything You Wanted to Know About Figuring Interest (Bringing Home the Gold Student Workouts.)*

✔ Small prizes for the assessment activity

LESSON DESCRIPTION

In order to compare the cost of different loans, students must understand finance charges and interest rates. In this lesson, the students learn how to compute finance charges, how to differentiate between add-on and annual percentage rates, and how the annual percentage rate and loan repayment period affect the cost of a loan.

This lesson is correlated with national standards for economics as well as the national guidelines for personal financial management as shown in Tables 1 and 2 in the front of this book.

PARENT CONNECTION

There is no specific family activity for this lesson, but there are activities in *The Parents' Guide* that parents might want to use with this lesson. These activities can be found in the "Raising the Bar" section for Theme 4.

The Parents' Guide is a tool for reinforcing and extending the instruction provided in the classroom. It includes:

1. Content background in the form of frequently asked questions.

2. Interesting activities that parents can do with their young adults.

3. An annotated listing of books and Internet resources related to each theme.

Student Objectives

At the end of this lesson the student will be able to:

✔ Describe the factors that determine the cost of credit.

✔ Describe the difference between an add-on and an annual percentage rate.

✔ Calculate finance charges using different interest rates.

✔ Calculate APRs given different finance charges and loan repayment periods.

✔ Analyze the relationships among the finance charge, principal of the loan, APR, and loan repayment period.

Workout

WARM-UP

Explain to the students that this is the beginning of a series of lessons that will help them shop for the lowest-cost loan. This lesson involves lots of math, but it is math that could help them save thousands of dollars in interest over their lifetime. Go figure and save big bucks.

EXERCISE

A. Ask the students to turn to Part I of Exercise 14.1, *Everything You Wanted to Know About Figuring Interest*. Go over with the students the formula FC=PRT, which is used to calculate finance charges. Have them complete Part I, questions 1-6, and go over the answers.

1. **Gabrielle Daily borrows $1,000 at a 6 percent add-on rate for one year. What is the finance charge?** *($60)*

2. **Jesse Candelaria borrows $2,000 at a 10 percent add-on rate for three years. What is the finance charge?** *($600)*

3. **Jessica Tate borrows $2,000 at a 10 percent add-on rate for two years. What is the finance charge?** *($400)*

4. **Travis Whitaker borrows $2,000 at an 8 percent add-on rate for two years. What is the finance charge?** *($320)*

5. **If you want to lower the finance charge, should you shop for a higher or lower interest rate?** *(Lower.)* **Why?** *(The interest will be less each year.)*

6. **If you want to lower the finance charge, should you pay back the loan more quickly or less quickly?** *(More quickly.)* **Why?** *(Because the amount of the loan outstanding for a period of time will be less because of your repayment.)*

B. Go over the formula MP=(P + I)/N, which is in Exercise 14.1. This formula is used to calculate the monthly payment on a loan. Have students complete Part II of Exercise 14.1, questions 1-5, and go over the answers.

1. **David Kim borrows $8,000 at an 8 percent add-on rate for two years. What is the interest?** *($1,280)* **What is the monthly payment?** *($386.67)*

2. **Maria Torres borrows $8,000 at an 8 percent add-on rate for four years. What is the interest?** *($2,560)* **What is the monthly payment?** *($220)*

3. **If a borrower takes longer to pay back a loan, what happens to the monthly payment?** *(It is lower.)*

4. **If a borrower takes longer to pay back a loan, what happens to the interest?** *(It is higher.)*

5. **What are the costs and benefits of taking longer to pay off a loan?** *(It is easier to make the monthly payments, but the cost is higher. In this case, the cost of the 48-month loan was $2,560, twice the cost of the 24-month loan.)*

C. Discuss the Truth in Lending Law and the formula for computing the APR in Part III. Because lenders must state the APR, students might think they shouldn't have to compute it. However, although the APR must be in a credit contract, lenders may state only an add-on rate or even a monthly rate. This is why students should understand exactly what an APR is. This is the purpose of this activity. Have the students answer Part III in Exercise 14.1, questions 1-3, and discuss the answers.

1. **Lisa Rosas borrows $5,000 at a 5 percent add-on rate for one year. What is the finance charge?** *($250)* **What is the APR?** *(9.2%)*

2. Brett Olson borrows $6,000 for three years at a 7 percent add-on rate. What is the finance charge? *($1,260)* **What is the APR?** *(13.6%)*

3. What is the relationship of an APR for an add-on rate for a one-payment loan compared to an add-on for a monthly installment loan? *(The APR is just less than double the add-on rate.)*

D. Ask the students the following questions to summarize the lesson.

1. What is the principal of a loan? *(The amount borrowed.)*

2. What is the finance charge on a loan? *(The amount of interest paid, stated in dollars.)*

3. What is the APR? Why is it important? *(APR stands for the annual percentage rate, which is the percentage of the principal that is paid in interest in a year. It is the best figure to use when comparing the cost of loans.)*

4. What is the difference between an APR and an add-on interest rate? *(An add-on rate assumes the borrower has the original principal of the loan for the entire loan period. An APR is calculated on the declining balance of the loan or only the principal that is still to be paid off.)*

5. How can a borrower lower the finance charge on a loan? *(Shop for a low APR and pay off the loan as quickly as possible.)*

COOL DOWN

Divide the class into teams of three students each. Project Visual 14.1. Show the problems and have the teams calculate the answers to all the problems. The winning team is the one which calculates the correct answers in the shortest period of time. Award that team a small prize. The answers to the problems are:

1. $240

2. $960

3. a) $1,680
b) $570

4. a) $1,350
b) $176.39
c) 17.5%

5. a) $3,000
b) $375
c) 9.8%

Other Training Equipment

An annotated bibliography and Internet resource list are available on our web site, **www.ncee.net**, as well as in *The Parents' Guide to Bringing Home the Gold*.

Financial Fitness for Life: Bringing Home the Gold Teacher Guide, ©National Council on Economic Education

Visual 14.1

Interest Rate Problems

1. JIM SMITH BORROWED $2,000 AT A
6% ADD-ON RATE FOR 2 YEARS.
   a. What is the finance charge?

2. ALEX ROLANDO BORROWED $4,000
AT AN 8% ADD-ON RATE FOR 3 YEARS.
   a. What is the finance charge?

3. ANN FONG BORROWED $12,000 AT A
7% ADD-ON RATE FOR 2 YEARS.
   a. What is the finance charge?
   b. What is the monthly payment?

4. MICHELLE WARD BORROWED $5,000
AT A 9% ADD-ON RATE FOR 3 YEARS.
   a. What is the finance charge?
   b. What is the monthly payment?
   c. What is the APR?

5. JULIE FRESHWATER BORROWED $15,000 AT A
5% ADD-ON RATE FOR 4 YEARS.
   a. What is the finance charge?
   b. What is the monthly payment?
   c. What is the APR?

75

LESSON

15

Shopping for a Credit Card

Fitness Focus

Make a transparency of the Visual.

✔ Visual 15.1, *Methods of Calculating Credit Card Interest*

✔ Exercise 15.1, *Comparing Credit Cards (Bringing Home the Gold Student Workouts)*

✔ Exercise 15.2, *Reading a Credit Card Statement (Bringing Home the Gold Student Workouts)*

✔ Family Activity 8, *Know the Options (The Parents' Guide to Bringing Home the Gold)*

✔ Family Activity 9, *What's Wrong with Just Paying the Minimum? (The Parents' Guide to Bringing Home the Gold)*

✔ Credit card solicitation letters and/or information sheets that accompany credit card statements.

LESSON DESCRIPTION

In 1999, 78 million households in the United States had a credit card, and Americans charged more than one trillion dollars on these cards. Many students believe that all credit cards are created equal. The first part of this lesson emphasizes that credit cards differ from one another in terms of annual fees, annual percentage rates, grace periods, and credit limits. In the second part of the lesson, students learn to read a credit card statement so they can see the real cost of charging goods and services.

This lesson is correlated with national standards for economics as well as the national guidelines for personal financial management as shown in Tables 1 and 2 in the front of the book.

PARENT CONNECTION

We recommend that two family activity worksheets be used with this lesson. Family Activity Worksheet 8 in *The Parents' Guide* encourages your students and their parents to compare and contrast characteristics of various credit card plans. This could be assigned as a pre-lesson activity or as a post-lesson activity. Having the students share the results with the class will demonstrate that all credit card offers are not the same.

The second activity, Family Activity 9, focuses on the results of paying only the required minimum on a credit card. This can be a fascinating discovery for both students

TIME REQUIRED

1 class period

and their parents. The answers to this paper-and-pencil activity are given in *The Parents' Guide*.

The Parents' Guide is a tool for reinforcing and extending the instruction provided in the classroom. It includes:

1. Content background in the form of frequently asked questions.
2. Interesting activities that parents can do with their young adults.
3. An annotated listing of books and Internet resources related to each theme.

Workout

WARM-UP

Ask the students how many of them have a credit card. Ask them what things they buy with their cards. If no students have credit cards, ask if they know of people who do, and what things they buy with their credit cards. *(Answers will vary, but may include such things as gas, clothing, CDs, small appliances, dinner at a restaurant, mail-order catalog purchases, and Internet purchases.)*

EXERCISE

A. Have the students read Exercise 15.1, *Comparing Credit Cards* in *Student Workouts*.

B. Show Visual 15.1, *Methods of Calculating Credit Card Interest*, and discuss how the three methods provide dissimilar interest for the month, even when the transactions are the same. Ask the students **which method is most favorable to the consumer; which method is most favorable to the creditor?** *(An adjusted balance method of calculation is usually more favorable to the cardholder than an average daily balance method. A previous balance method is usually most favorable to the creditor.)*

C. Have the students answer the question in Exercise 15.1, and discuss the answer.

  1. What characteristics should you look for if you want to save money on a credit card? *(The credit card should have a low fee or no annual fee, a low APR, and a long grace period.)*

D. Go over Exercise 15.2, *Reading a Credit Card Statement* in *Student Workouts*.

Student Objectives

At the end of this lesson the student will be able to:

✔ Describe how credit cards differ in terms of the annual fee, annual percentage rate, grace period, and credit limit.

✔ Read and understand a credit card statement.

✔ Evaluate the costs and benefits of using a credit card to purchase goods and services.

E. Have the students answer the questions about the statement, and discuss them.

  1. How much did Tim Gray charge in the month of the statement? *($30.63)*

  2. Did Tim make a payment in the previous month? If so, how much was the payment? *(He did not make a payment.)*

  3. What is the total credit available on this credit card? *($7,500)*

  4. How much of that credit was available at the time of this statement? *($6,336)*

5. How does Tim's previous balance compare to the new balance shown on this statement? *(The new balance is $51.87 higher than the previous balance.)*

6. Was Tim charged a finance charge this month? If so, what was the amount of the finance charge? *(Yes. He was charged a finance charge of $21.24 this month.)*

7. What is the annual percentage rate that Tim pays for credit on this account? *(21%)*

8. Looking at this statement, do you think Tim is handling his credit well? Why or why not? What would you recommend? *(Tim is not handling his credit well. He is not paying off his monthly balance. In fact, his monthly balance is increasing. He is paying a relatively high APR. Tim should consider how he could quickly pay off the total balance of this card.)*

COOL DOWN

Ask the students to bring to class credit card solicitation letters or the information sheets that accompany credit card statements. An alternative to collecting solicitation letters is to compare credit cards online. One web site, **www.bankrate.com,** could be useful. Put the students in groups of three and have them compare the features of three different credit cards. Students should use the following chart to make their comparisons. Or have the students do this same activity, which is in *The Parents' Guide* (see Parent Connection), with their family members.

	Card 1	Card 2	Card 3
Name of company			
Annual fee			
APR			
Grace period			
Credit limit			
Minimum payment			
Penalties (late fee)			

After completing the chart, the students should rank the cards from best to worst from a cardholder's perspective.

Other Training Equipment

An annotated bibliography and Internet resource list are available on our web site, **www.ncee.net**, as well as in *The Parents' Guide to Bringing Home the Gold.*

Financial Fitness for Life: Bringing Home the Gold Teacher Guide, ©National Council on Economic Education

Visual 15.1

Methods of Calculating Credit Card Interest

Assume an APR of 18.9% and a daily interest rate of .05476% (.0005476). For these examples the number of days in the cycle is 30, and only payments have been included.

An actual active account with purchases or cash advances would be more involved.

April 1 Opening balance $1,000
April 15 Payment   400
April 30 Closing balance   600

AVERAGE DAILY BALANCE:

You pay interest on the average balance owed during the billing cycle. The creditor figures the balance in your account on each day of the billing cycle, then adds together these amounts and divides by the number of days in the billing cycle.

Average balance = $1000 x 15 days x .0005476 = $8.21
$ 600 x 15 days x .0005476 =   4.93
$13.14

ADJUSTED BALANCE:

You pay interest on the opening balance after subtracting the payment or returns made during the month.

Opening balance = $1,000
Payment   400
Interest calculated on 600 x 30 x .0005476 = $9.86

PREVIOUS BALANCE:

You pay interest on the opening balance, regardless of payments made during the month.

Opening balance = $1,000 X 30 X .0005476 = $16.43

Financial Fitness for Life: Bringing Home the Gold Teacher Guide, ©National Council on Economic Education

LESSON

16

Shopping for a Mortgage

Welcome to
Loan Calculator 1.1

Click here to begin

Fitness Focus

EQUIPMENT AND GETTING READY!

✔ Exercise 16.1, *Using the Computer to Calculate Payments for a Loan (Bringing Home the Gold Student Workouts)*

✔ A computer or more ideally a computer lab with Internet access; or a computer with a mortgage calculator on the hard drive

TIME REQUIRED
1 class period.

LESSON DESCRIPTION

In this lesson, students use a computer loan calculator to determine the cost of a loan. This technique is particularly important for mortgage calculations. There are many loan calculators on the Internet, and many software packages, such as *Quicken,* also contain loan calculators.

This lesson is correlated with national standards for economics as well as the national guidelines for personal financial management as shown in Tables 1 and 2 in the front of this book.

PARENT CONNECTION

There is no specific family activity for this lesson, but there are activities in *The Parents' Guide* that parents might want to use with this lesson. These activities can be found in the "Raising the Bar" section for Theme 4.

The Parents' Guide is a tool for reinforcing and extending the instruction provided in the classroom. It includes:

1. Content background in the form of frequently asked questions.
2. Interesting activities that parents can do with their young adults.
3. An annotated listing of books and Internet resources related to each theme.

Student Objectives

At the end of this lesson the student will be able to:

✔ Describe what it means to amortize a loan.

✔ Use a computer program to amortize several mortgages.

✔ Describe how the cost of buying a home on credit can be reduced.

Workout

WARM-UP

Tell the students that in this lesson they will learn how they can use a loan or mortgage calculator to amortize the cost of a loan.

EXERCISE

A. Have the students turn to Exercise 16.1, *Using a Computer to Calculate Payments for a Loan,* and complete the Mortgage Chart. This gives students practice in using an amortization program. Because an APR is based on the declining value of a loan, an amortization program is needed to calculate interest and monthly payments. There are many amortization programs on the Internet. The web site, www.mortgagesto-go.com/calculators.asp, is one that can be used. Have the students complete the activity and answer the questions.

Exercise 16.1 Answers to Mortgage Chart

	Mortgage 1	**Mortgage 2**	**Mortgage 3**	**Mortgage 4**
Home price	$125,000	$125,000	$125,000	$125,000
Down payment %	20%	5%	20%	20%
Down payment $	$25,000	$6,250	$25,000	$25,000
Principal	$100,000	$118,750	$100,000	$100,000
Annual interest rate	7%	5%	6%	6.5%
Term	30 years	30 years	30 years	15 years
Monthly payment	$665.30	$790.71	$599.55	$871.11
Total interest	$139,508.90	$165,806.33	$115,838.19	$56,799.33
Total payments (down payment, principal, and interest)	$264,508.90	$290,806.33	$240,838.19	$181,799.33

B. Discuss the answers to the questions in Exercise 16.1 that follow the chart.

1. What happens to the monthly payment and total payment for a loan with a smaller down payment? *(Both the monthly payment and the total payment are higher.)*

2. What happens to the monthly payment and total payment for a loan with a lower annual interest rate? *(Both the monthly payment and the total payment are less.)*

3. What happens to the monthly payment and total payment if the term of the mortgage is 15 years rather than 30 years? *(You pay more each month, which can be tough on the budget. However, you save a lot on interest, so the total payment is less.)*

4. What is the trade-off if you get a 15-year mortgage rather than a 30-year mortgage? *(With a 15-year mortgage, you pay lower total interest but trade-off the lower monthly payments of a 30-year mortgage.)*

81

5. How can you reduce your cost of buying a home? *(Increase the down payment, pay the mortgage off faster, and find a lower APR.)*

COOL DOWN

Use a different set of amortization problems as a test.

Other Training Equipment

An annotated bibliography and Internet resource list are available on our web site, **www.ncee.net**, as well as in *The Parents' Guide to Bringing Home the Gold.*

LESSON

17

Shopping for an Auto Loan

Fitness Focus

EQUIPMENT AND GETTING READY!

- Exercise 17.1, *Getting the Best Deal on Your Auto Loan (Bringing Home the Gold Student Workouts)*

- Exercise 17.2, *Shopping Online for an Auto Loan (Bringing Home the Gold Student Workouts)*

- Exercise 17.3, *Shopping in Your Community for an Auto Loan (Bringing Home the Gold Student Workouts)*

- Family Activity 10, *What Does It Cost to Finance a Car? (The Parents' Guide to Bringing Home the Gold)*

- A computer or computer lab with Internet access

TIME REQUIRED

1 and one-half class periods.

8 The online and local shopping activities could be done in class or assigned as homework.

LESSON DESCRIPTION

Consumers must shop for credit just as they do for a car or a computer. In this lesson, students learn the skills they need to shop for credit by filling out a credit comparison chart for a hypothetical loan. Then, using the same techniques, they shop online for a loan. Finally, students compare the cost of the same loan at local lending institutions.

This lesson is correlated with national standards for economics as well as the national guidelines for personal financial management as shown in Tables 1 and 2 in the front of the book.

PARENT CONNECTION

We recommend one family activity worksheet be used with this lesson. Family Activity Worksheet 10 in *The Parents' Guide* has the student select an automobile and then comparison shop with his or her parents for a loan for that purchase. Students can share the results of their shopping experiences in class to show the variety of plans available for financing an auto purchase.

The Parents' Guide is a tool for reinforcing and extending the instruction provided in the classroom. It includes:

1. Content background in the form of frequently asked questions.

2. Interesting activities that parents can do with their young adults.

3. An annotated listing of books and Internet resources related to each theme.

Workout

WARM-UP

Explain to the students that it is easy to shop for a loan. Money is money. The lowest-cost loan is the best deal. To shop for a loan, a borrower must first decide on the type of loan, the amount to be borrowed (principal of the loan), and the number of years to repay the loan. Then the borrower should shop for the loan with the lowest APR. The lowest APR should also have the lowest finance charge (cost of the loan). If it does not, the borrower has been given incorrect information.

At the end of this lesson the student will be able to:

✔ Compare and contrast the cost of different loans and choose the loan with the lowest cost.

✔ Shop for a loan online.

✔ Evaluate the factors that reduce the cost of a loan.

EXERCISE

A. Discuss with the students some of the mistakes people make in shopping for a loan.

- **Mistake 1:** Looking for the lowest monthly payments. The longer the repayment period, the higher the finance charge. Don't focus on the monthly payments.

- **Mistake 2:** Not asking for the identical principal and repayment schedule. Always compare the cost of the same loan. Don't try to compare apples and oranges.

- **Mistake 3:** Not asking for both the APR and finance charge. By asking for both, you will be sure the information given is correct.

B. Have the students read Exercise 17.1 in *Student Workouts* and do the activities. Go over the chart and the answers to the questions.

Name of Place	APR	Finance Charge	Total Cost	Monthly Payment
Last National Bank	7.49 %	$1,434.90	$13,434.90	$373.19
Online lending site	8.41 %	$1,619.17	$13,619.17	$378.31
Car dealer	9.50 %	$1,838.23	$13,838.23	$384.40
Friendly Finance Company	13.95 %	$2,754.25	$14,754.25	$409.84

1. Which loan is the best deal? *(Last National Bank.)*

2. Which loan is the worst deal? *(Friendly Finance Company.)*

3. Jill took the best loan. How much extra did she pay because she financed her car instead of buying it for cash? *($1,434.90)*

4. How much money did Jill save by taking the best deal rather than the worst deal? *($1,319.35)*

C. Have the students complete Exercise 17.2, *Shopping Online for an Auto Loan.* (This exercise requires Internet access.) Here are some suggestions for conducting the activity.

1. Because online lending sources are constantly changing, students should conduct a search. The key is to narrow the search. For example, a search for "loans" yielded 12,351 sites. A search for "loans + credit" yielded 3,894 sites. A search for "loan rate comparisons" yielded 253 sites. You could also visit the web sites of major banks, savings and loans, and credit unions to complete this activity.

2. Most of the web sites will provide information without requiring the students to sign up. Make sure they do not provide their name, address, or, most importantly, Social Security number for any site. The students are making comparisons, not actually getting a loan.

D. Have the students complete the activity .

E. Discuss the answers to the questions. Find out how much money was saved by selecting the best offer rather than the worst offer the class found.

F. Now have the students complete Exercise 17.3, *Shopping in Your Community for an Auto Loan.* You can assign this activity as a group or individual project. You might also want to assign this as a family project. Family Activity 9 in *The Parents' Guide* is similar to this activity.

1. Have the students make a list of some of the banks, savings and loans, and credit unions in your area.

2. Have the students call four lending institutions, ask for a loan officer, and find out the APR and finance charge for the loan. You could also have them ask if there are any additional fees that might add to the cost. Finally, have them find out if checking or savings account customers might qualify for a lower rate.

3. Have the students fill in the chart and answer the questions.

4. Discuss the answers to the questions.
- For questions 1-5, the answers will vary depending on the gathered data.

- For question 6, possible answers could include:
  Advantages—Local institutions may offer more assistance and personal attention than online shopping.

  Disadvantages—The Internet provides greater choice of auto loans. The Internet is available 24 hours a day—local institutions are not.

85

COOL DOWN

Have the students fill out a credit comparison sheet for a different loan. Change the amount of the loan and the repayment period. Also change the purpose of the loan; the students could shop for a college loan or a *used* car loan.

Other Training Equipment

An annotated bibliography and Internet resource list are available on our web site, **www.ncee.net**, as well as in *The Parents' Guide to Bringing Home the Gold.*

LESSON

18

Consumer Credit Protection

EQUIPMENT AND GETTING READY!

Make a transparency of the Visual.

Visual 18.1, *Questions for Credit Counselors*

Exercise 18.1, *Consumer Credit Protection (Bringing Home the Gold Student Workouts)*

Exercise 18.2, *Credible Credit Counselors (Bringing Home the Gold Student Workouts)*

Exercise 18.3, *Legal Protection for Borrowers (Bringing Home the Gold Student Workouts)*

TIME REQUIRED
1 class period.

Fitness Focus

LESSON DESCRIPTION

This lesson provides an overview of consumer credit protection. It stresses the federal laws designed to protect credit consumers from lenders' mistakes. These include the *Truth in Lending Act, Fair Credit Reporting Act, Equal Credit Opportunity Act, Fair Credit Billing Act, Fair Debt Collection Practices Act*, and, most recently, the *Electronic Fund Transfer Act*.

This lesson is correlated with national standards for economics as well as the national guidelines for personal financial management as shown in Tables 1 and 2 in the front of this book.

PARENT CONNECTION

There is no specific family activity for this lesson, but there are activities in *The Parents' Guide* that parents might want to use with this lesson. These activities can be found in the "Raising the Bar" section for Theme 4.

The Parents' Guide is a tool for reinforcing and extending the instruction provided in the classroom.It includes:

1. Content background in the form of frequently asked questions.

2. Interesting activities that parents can do with their young adults.

3. An annotated listing of books and Internet resources related to each theme.

Workout

WARM-UP

Explain that the purpose of this lesson is to help the students identify legislation that offers consumers credit protection.

EXERCISE

A. Ask the students to turn to Exercise 18.1, *Consumer Credit Protection* in *Student Workouts*. After the students have completed the reading, discuss the questions related to that section.

1. **What credit problems are common among young adults?** *(Young adults might live beyond their means. Excessive credit card debt is a common problem.)*

2. **What are common causes of credit problems among other age groups?** *(An unexpected illness, loss of a job, divorce, or loss of child care are some of the factors that might cause financial trouble.)*

3. **What levels of government offer consumer credit protection?** *(State and federal.)*

4. **Why do most credit transactions benefit both the borrower and the lender?** *(The vast majority of credit transactions involve mutual gains. The borrower is able to purchase something now that may have value today and perhaps in the future. The lender is repaid the money that was loaned, plus interest.)*

5. **What act protects consumers from unauthorized use of credit cards?** *(The Truth in Lending Act.)*

6. **What act forbids collection agencies from using harassment to collect debts?** *(The Fair Debt Collection Practices Act.)*

Student Objectives

At the end of this lesson the student will be able to:

✔ Identify features of key federal legislation that help protect consumers in credit transactions.

✔ Analyze how key federal credit legislation applies to specific credit problems.

7. **What act requires creditors to bill you at least 14 days before payment is due?** *(The Fair Credit Billing Act.)*

8. **What act protects credit consumers against discrimination on the basis of sex or race?** *(The Equal Credit Opportunity Act.)*

9. **What act sets a process for consumers to correct inaccuracies in their credit report?** *(The Fair Credit Reporting Act.)*

10. **What act offers some protection when using a debit card?** *(The Electronic Fund Transfer Act.)*

B. Explain that the students are going to play the role of credit counselors. Direct the students' attention to Exercise 18.2, *Credible Credit Counselors*. Read Part I that explains the purpose of *Credible Credit Counselors*. Divide the class into small groups. Ask the students in each group to read one or two of the situations of the six clients in Part II. The groups should answer the questions in Part I for each client. Use Visual 18.1, *Questions for Credit Counselors*.

C. After the students have read and discussed the cases, discuss their recommendations with the whole class.

Client 1

1. According to federal law, what are the legal rights of your client? *(The Electronic Fund Transfer Act limits the client's loss to $50 because the cardholder contacted the card issuer immediately after discovering the loss.)*

2. Are your client's legal rights being violated? *(The client is a victim of a crime but has protection of federal laws.)*

3. Is your client being responsible or irresponsible? *(The client is acting in a responsible manner.)*

4. What should your client do? *(Cancel the debit card immediately. Continue to work with the card issuer until the matter is resolved.)*

Client 2

1. According to federal law, what are the legal rights of your client? *(The telephone calls your client is getting from the collection agency may constitute harassment that is a violation of the Fair Debt Collection Practices Act.)*

2. Are your client's legal rights being violated? *(Probably. The telephone calls may be illegal.)*

3. Is your client being responsible or irresponsible? *(The client was acting irresponsibly by not paying the loan as agreed.)*

4. What should your client do? *(The client may wish to contact federal authorities to end the harassment under the Fair Debt Collection Practices Act. The client should immediately contact the agency and try to work out a mutually agreeable repayment plan.)*

Client 3

1. According to federal law, what are the legal rights of your client? *(The client has a right under the Truth in Lending Act to know all the terms of credit. If the amount of a payment is mentioned in an advertisement, all other credit terms must be disclosed.)*

2. Are your client's legal rights being violated? *(Yes, your client's rights are being violated along with the rights of other consumers.)*

3. Is your client being responsible or irresponsible? *(The client is acting in a responsible manner.)*

4. What should your client do? *(The client might want to alert the company running the ad or bring the ad to the attention of federal authorities. Tell the client to look elsewhere for a sofa.)*

Client 4

1. According to federal law, what are the legal rights of your client? *(The client has a right under the Equal Credit Opportunity Act to know the reason for the denial of a loan.)*

2. Are your client's legal rights being violated? *(Yes. The reason for denial was not provided. We are unable to tell if the creditor is discriminating against the client on the basis of marital status, race, age, gender, etc.)*

3. Is your client being responsible or irresponsible? *(The client is acting in a responsible manner.)*

4. What should your client do? *(The client should contact the company immediately and ask for a reason for the denial. The client may wish to file a formal complaint with the federal authorities if there is evidence of discrimination.)*

Client 5

1. **According to federal law, what are the legal rights of your client?** *(The Truth in Lending Act limits liability for unauthorized charges prior to notifying the credit card company of the lost card.)*

2. **Are your client's legal rights being violated?** *(No. It appears that no rights are being violated.)*

3. **Is your client being responsible or irresponsible?** *(Client 5 is shirking his or her responsibility to contact the credit card company immediately, so that the company can close the account and stop all new charges.)*

4. **What should your client do?** *(Client 5 should contact the credit card company immediately.)*

Client 6

1. **According to federal law, what are the legal rights of your client?** *(The client has a right under the Truth in Lending Act that creditors present borrowers with an annual percentage rate [APR] for all the costs of financing, including any loan fees.)*

2. **Are your client's legal rights being violated?** *(Yes. The lender is required to supply the APR information.)*

3. **Is your client being responsible or irresponsible?** *(The client is acting in a responsible manner.)*

4. **What should your client do?** *(The client should contact the car dealership immediately and bring this matter to its attention. The client may wish to file a formal complaint with the federal authorities. Tell the client to look elsewhere for a car.)*

D. Review the key points of this lesson. Ask:

1. **Who gains from credit transactions?** *(Almost always, both sides benefit in a credit transaction. Borrowers are able to purchase something that may be of value today and perhaps in the future. Lenders are repaid the money that was loaned plus interest.)*

2. **Name the federal laws examined in this lesson that regulate consumer credit.** *(Electronic Fund Transfer Act, Equal Credit Opportunity Act, Fair Credit Billing Act, Fair Debt Collection Practices Act, Fair Credit Reporting Act, Truth in Lending Act.)*

COOL DOWN

Ask the students to open to Exercise 18.3, *Legal Protection for Borrowers* in *Student Workouts.* Tell the students to complete the chart. You may wish to have the students discuss their answers.

STATEMENT 1	**Fair Debt Collection Practices Act**
STATEMENT 2	**Equal Credit Opportunity Act**
STATEMENT 3	**Truth in Lending Act**
STATEMENT 4	**Equal Credit Opportunity Act**
STATEMENT 5	**Fair Credit Reporting Act**
STATEMENT 6	**Fair Credit Reporting Act**
STATEMENT 7	**Electronic Fund Transfer Act**
STATEMENT 8	**Fair Credit Billing Act**
STATEMENT 9	**Truth in Lending Act**

Other Training Equipment

An annotated bibliography and Internet resource list are available on our web site, **www.ncee.net**, as well as in *The Parents' Guide to Bringing Home the Gold.*

91

Visual 18.1

Questions for Credit Counselors

Instructions:

After reading each client's case, answer the following questions.

1. According to federal law, what are the legal rights of your client?

2. Are your client's rights being violated?

3. Is your client acting in a responsible or irresponsible way?

4. What should your client do?

Financial Fitness for Life: Bringing Home the Gold Teacher Guide, ©National Council on Economic Education

LESSON

19

Scams and Schemes

Fitness Focus

EQUIPMENT AND GETTING READY!

Make a transparency of the Visual.

- Visual 19.1, *Steps to Reduce the Chance of Identity Theft*

- Exercise 19.1, *Scams and Schemes (Bringing Home the Gold Student Workouts)*

- Exercise 19.2, *Name That Scam (Bringing Home the Gold Student Workouts)*

TIME REQUIRED

1 and one-half class periods.

LESSON DESCRIPTION

This lesson reminds students that while most credit transactions are completely legal, there are some that are not. This lesson introduces scams and schemes, such as identify theft, loan scams, and credit repair loans. The lesson also features legal but high-cost credit practices prevalent in urban areas such as payday loans and rent-to-own plans.

This lesson is correlated with national standards for economics as well as the national guidelines for personal financial management as shown in Tables 1 and 2 in the front of this book.

PARENT CONNECTION

There is no specific family activity for this lesson, but there are activities in *The Parents' Guide* that parents might want to use with this lesson. These activities can be found in the "Raising the Bar" section for Theme 4.

The Parents' Guide is a tool for reinforcing and extending the instruction provided in the classroom. It includes:

1. Content background in the form of frequently asked questions.
2. Interesting activities that parents can do with their young adults.
3. An annotated listing of books and Internet resources related to each theme.

Student Objectives

At the end of this lesson the student will be able to:

✔ Recognize various forms of consumer credit frauds.

✔ Identify high-cost credit practices.

Workout

WARM-UP

Tell the class that each year millions of consumers are involved in credit scams and schemes. Explain that the purpose of this lesson is to explain some common credit scams and schemes and ways to avoid them.

EXERCISE

A. Direct the students' attention to Exercise 19.1, *Scams and Schemes* in *Student Workouts*. After the students have read these pages, ask them to complete the chart in which they match definitions to the name of the scam. Discuss their answers.

Scam or Scheme	Definition
Rent-to-own	G
Credit repair scheme	A
College financial aid scam	B
Pyramid schemes	F
Payday loan	E
Identity theft	C
Loan scam	D

B. Explain to the class that there are ways to avoid scams and schemes. Stress the idea that the buyer should beware. Although there are laws to protect you, being a careful and skeptical consumer is the best way to avoid trouble. When a deal sounds too good to be true, it is. Ask questions. Hang up on the telemarketer offering the chance of a lifetime to buy a gold mine. Walk away from the salesperson on a college campus that offers you a free trip to Cancun in exchange for your credit card or debit card number.

C. Stress the importance of families living within or below their means. When people live at or below their means, it is easier to avoid seeking credit that involves high interest rates like the ones charged for payday loans. Living at or below their means will allow individuals to apply to banks, credit unions, and other conventional credit-offering institutions for credit. These institutions charge "normal" market rates when people seek credit.

D. Point out that there are other steps that can be taken to avoid scams and swindles. Display Visual 19.1 and discuss some of the suggestions for avoiding identity scams.

E. Review some of the key points in this lesson. Ask:

1. **Name the scams and schemes examined in this lesson.** *(Identity theft, loan scam, credit repair loan scheme, college financial aid scam, pyramid scheme, payday loan, rent-to-own.)*

COOL DOWN

Direct the students' attention to Exercise 19.2, *Name That Scam* in *Student Workouts*. Read each scam and have the students identify and explain the type of scan.

SCAM 1 **is E, a pyramid scam.**

SCAM 2 **is F, a payday loan.**

SCAM 3 **is G, a rent-to-own scheme.**

SCAM 4 **is E, a pyramid scam.**

SCAM 5 **is A, an identity theft.**

SCAM 6 **is C, a credit repair scheme.**

SCAM 7 **is B, a loan scam.**

SCAM 8 **is D, a college financial aid scam.**

Other Training Equipment

An annotated bibliography and Internet resource list are available on our web site, **www.ncee.net**, as well as in *The Parents' Guide to Bringing Home the Gold.*

Visual 19.1

Steps to Reduce the Chance of Identity Theft

☞ Sign your credit or debit cards as soon as they arrive.

☞ Carry your cards in a safe place separately from your wallet.

☞ Keep a record of your account numbers, their expiration dates, and the phone number and address of each company in a secure place.

☞ Keep an eye on your card during a transaction.

☞ Destroy carbons.

☞ Save receipts to compare with billing statements.

☞ Open bills promptly and reconcile accounts monthly, just as you would your checking account.

☞ Report any questionable charges promptly and in writing to the card issuer.

☞ Do not lend your card(s) to anyone.

☞ Do not leave cards or receipts lying around.

☞ Do not sign a blank receipt. When you sign a receipt, draw a line through any blank spaces above the total.

☞ Do not give out your account number over the phone unless you're making the call to a company you know is reputable.

☞ If you lose your credit or debit cards, or if you realize they've been stolen, immediately contact the issuer of the card.

Get a Plan:
Get a Grip on Life
OVERVIEW

This final unit introduces students to the topics of money management strategies, banking practices, and insurance.

Lesson 20

provides a radio call-in show format to introduce the students to family budgeting and the distinction between income and net worth. To practice making budgeting decisions, the students make spending recommendations for a young family.

Lesson 21

explains four types of financial institutions: commercial banks, savings and loans, credit unions, and brokerage firms. The students investigate the types of services available from financial institutions in their own community. As an example of a common financial service, the lesson stresses the basics of using a checking account, such as how to write a check, make a deposit, and reconcile a checking account.

Lesson 22

stresses the idea that there are no risk-free choices. It explains how insurance works using school lockers as an example. It provides an overview of the different types of insurance including auto, health, renter's, homeowner's, life, and disability. Students participate in a simulation that allows them to practice their understanding of the costs and benefits associated with purchasing insurance.

LESSON

20

Managing Your Money

Fitness Focus

EQUIPMENT AND GETTING READY!

✔ Theme 5 *Student Letter* and *Frequently Asked Questions* (*Bringing Home the Gold Student Workouts*)

✔ Exercise 20.1, *Budgets Are Beautiful Call-In Show* (*Bringing Home the Gold Student Workouts*)

✔ Exercise 20.2A, *John and Marcia: Monthly Spending Plan 1* (*Bringing Home the Gold Student Workouts*)

✔ Exercise 20.2B, *John and Marcia: Monthly Spending Plan 2* (*Bringing Home the Gold Student Workouts*)

LESSON DESCRIPTION

This lesson introduces some of the basics of money management. By means of a radio call-in show script, students learn about setting up a family budget and distinguishing between income and net worth. To practice making budgeting decisions, the students make spending recommendations for a young family.

This lesson is correlated with national standards for economics as well as the national guidelines for personal financial management as shown in Tables 1 and 2 in the front of this book.

PARENT CONNECTION

There is no specific family activity for this lesson, but there are activities in *The Parents' Guide* that parents might want to use with this lesson. These activities can be found in the "Raising the Bar" section for Theme 5.

The Parents' Guide is a tool for reinforcing and extending the instruction provided in the classroom. It includes:

TIME REQUIRED
2 class periods.

1. Content background in the form of frequently asked questions.

2. Interesting activities that parents can do with their young adults.

3. An annotated listing of books and Internet resources related to each theme.

Workout

WARM-UP

A. Have the students read the Student Letter for Theme 5 in *Student Workouts* and discuss the questions.

Answers to the Student Letter Questions

1. What is a budget? *(A budget is a device for keeping track of your income and expenses. It involves making a list of your income and expenses. After making the list, you subtract your expenses from your income. If you have any surplus cash, you can plan how you will use it.)*

2. What are examples of financial institutions? *(Important financial institutions are commercial banks, savings and loans, credit unions, and brokerage firms.)*

3. What is the point of buying insurance? *(Insurance is a way of reducing risk.)*

4. What are common forms of insurance? *(Auto, health, renter's, homeowner's, life, and disability.)*

5. When is the best time to get started on saving your first million bucks? *(Now.)*

B. Explain that the purpose of this lesson is to help the students understand key aspects of financial planning including managing a family budget and calculating net worth.

Student Objectives

At the end of this lesson the student will be able to:

✔ Identify key terms such as disposable income, family budget, variable expense, fixed expense, and net worth.

✔ Identify the characteristics of a typical monthly family budget including income, expenses, and savings.

✔ Make spending recommendations for a fictional young family, recognizing the costs and the benefits involved.

EXERCISE

A. Stress the idea that decisions made regarding the use of your income are similar to other choices. There are advantages and disadvantages to various spending decisions. Sacrifices can be difficult to make when the costs must be paid in the short term and most of the benefits occur in the future.

B. Have the students turn to Exercise 20.1, *Budgets Are Beautiful Call-In Show* in *Student Workouts*. Ask five students to take the roles of Budget Bob, Dr. Penny Saver, Connie from Connecticut, Calvin from California, and Minnie from Minnesota. Have the students read the script of the *Budgets Are*

Beautiful Call-In Show. Ask the students to answer the questions that follow the script. Discuss the answers.

1. What is disposable income? *(Disposable income is the money that you have to spend or save as you wish after deductions [e.g., taxes, Social Security, and other items of your choice] have been taken out of your gross pay.)*

2. What does Dr. Saver recommend as the three parts of a family budget? *(A family budget should include a listing of income, expenses, and savings.)*

3. What are fixed and variable expenses? Use examples to illustrate each. *(Fixed expenses are ones that are relatively constant each month, such as a house payment, rent payment, and car payment. Variable expenses are ones that are likely to change or can be changed in the short term. Telephone bills, groceries, medical bills not covered by insurance, entertainment, recreation, and charge account purchases are examples.)*

4. What does this idea of "pay yourself first" mean? *(Some savers include their savings goal in the fixed expenses part of their budget.)*

5. What is net worth? *(Net worth is a way of measuring wealth. It is the current value of assets minus liabilities. [Liabilities are debts you owe.])*

C. Direct the students' attention to Exercise 20.2A, *John and Marcia: Spending Plan 1* in *Student Workouts*. Ask the class to read the background information regarding John and Marcia. Ask:

1. Who are John and Marcia? *(A young, married couple working to support one child.)*

2. What is their lifestyle? *(They live in a comfortable apartment, enjoy some small luxuries, and keep up with all their bills.)*

3. What is their immediate financial goal? *(To save enough money for a down payment on a second car.)*

D. Ask the students to examine the part of Exercise 20.2A that shows Marcia and John's fixed and variable expenses for Spending Plan 1. Ask the class to make their recommendations about how John and Marcia might reduce their variable expenses to achieve the saving goal they have established to purchase a second car. Ask the students to answer the questions which appear after the budgets. Discuss the answers.

1. What are some examples of John and Marcia's fixed expenses? *(Housing, health insurance, life and disability insurance, renter's insurance, automobile insurance, college loan, etc.)*

2. What are some examples of John and Marcia's variable expenses? *(Meals, utilities, automobile fuel, medical, child care, clothing, etc.)*

3. John and Marcia have decided to practice the "pay yourself first" approach to saving for a second car. How do they pay themselves first? *(They have the amount that they want to save taken out of their pay before they receive their paychecks).*

4. Examine the monthly spending plan above. What sacrifices do you think John and Marcia should make in their variable expenses to meet their goal? *(Answers will vary. Accept any reasonable answers.*

5. What are the benefits and costs of your recommended decisions for John and Marcia? *(The benefit is that the combination of choices will allow John and Marcia to obtain the second car they want. The cost is giving up the things they would like to do and have right now, so they can save more.)*

E. Review some of the key points in this lesson. Ask:

1. **What is disposable income?** *(Disposable income is the money that you have left after you pay your taxes, Social Security, and the other deductions that have been taken out of gross pay.)*

2. **What does Dr. Saver recommend for the three parts of a family budget?** *(A family budget should include a listing of income and expenses plus a plan for saving.)*

3. **What are fixed expenses? Use examples to illustrate each.** *(Fixed expenses are ones that are relatively constant each month, such as a house payment, rent payment, and car payment. Experts in personal finance believe savings should be a fixed expense.)*

4. **What are variable expenses?** *(Variable expenses are ones that are likely to change in the short term. Telephone bills, groceries, medical bills not covered by insurance, entertainment, recreation, and charge account purchases are examples.)*

5. **What is net worth?** *(Net worth is the current value of assets minus liabilities.)*

6. **What sorts of sacrifices did you advise Marcia and John to make to save for their second car?** *(Answers will vary.)*

COOL DOWN

Ask the students to examine Exercise 20.2B. It shows Marcia and John's fixed and variable expenses for Spending Plan 2. In this new situation, John and Marcia want to set aside their savings toward a home down payment fund. Ask the class to make their recommendations about how John and Marcia might reduce their expenses to achieve the goal of saving for a home. Ask the students to answer the questions that follow the income and spending plan. Discuss the answers.

1. **What is John and Marcia's new financial goal?** *(Saving for their first home.)*

2. **Examine the monthly spending plan above. What sacrifices do you think John and Marcia should make in their variable expenses to meet their goal?** *(Answers will vary. Accept any reasonable answers.)*

3. **What are the benefits and costs of your recommended decisions for John and Marcia?** *(The benefit is that the combination of choices will allow John and Marcia to become future homeowners. The cost is sacrificing things they would like to do and have right now.)*

Other Training Equipment

An annotated bibliography and Internet resource list are available on our web site, **www.ncee.net**, as well as in *The Parents' Guide to Bringing Home the Gold.*

Financial Fitness for Life: Bringing Home the Gold Teacher Guide, ©National Council on Economic Education

LESSON

21

Banking Basics

Fitness Focus

EQUIPMENT AND GETTING READY!

Make a transparency of the Visual.

✔ Visual 21.1, *Bank Register Answer Key*

✔ Exercise 21.1, *What Are Financial Institutions? (Bringing Home the Gold Workouts)*

✔ Exercise 21.2, *Checking Out Checking Accounts (Bringing Home the Gold Student Workouts)*

✔ Exercise 21.3, *Keeping a Checking Account (Bringing Home the Gold Student Workouts)*

✔ Exercise 21.4, *Financial Services Survey (Bringing Home the Gold Student Workouts)*

✔ Illustration 21.1, *A Completed Deposit Ticket (Bringing Home the Gold Student Workouts)*

✔ Illustration 21.2, *The Finer Points of Writing a Check (Bringing Home the Gold Student Workouts)*

✔ Family Activity 11, *Researching Checking Accounts (The Parents' Guide to Bringing Home the Gold)*

✔ Family Activity 12, *$2000 Computer! $0 Down! 0% a Month! For Six Months! (The Parents' Guide to Bringing Home the Gold)*

LESSON DESCRIPTION

This lesson provides an overview of four types of financial institutions. It invites the students to investigate services available from financial institutions in their own community. As an example of a common financial service, the lesson stresses the basics of using a checking account.

This lesson is correlated with national standards for economics as well as the national guidelines for personal financial management as shown in Tables 1 and 2 in the front of the book.

PARENT CONNECTION

We recommend two family activity worksheets be used with this lesson. Family Activity Worksheet 11 in *The Parents' Guide* encourages your students to comparison shop with their parents for a checking account.

Having students bring in the results will demonstrate the variety of checking accounts plans available in the community.

Student Objectives

At the end of this lesson the student will be able to:

✔ Recognize the key deposit, credit, and investment services offered by commercial banks, savings and loans, credit unions, and brokerage firms.

✔ Identify different types of checking accounts.

✔ Recognize the steps in setting up and managing a checking account.

✔ Differentiate between the uses of an ATM and a debit card.

Family Activity 12 suggests a way to analyze the worth of a computer offer with a checking account. The lesson focuses on one of the many "added features" found in checking account offers.

The Parents' Guide is a tool for reinforcing and extending the instruction provided in the classroom. It includes:

1. Content background in the form of frequently asked questions.

2. Interesting activities that parents can do with their young adults.

3. An annotated listing of books and Internet resources related to each theme.

Workout

WARM-UP

Explain that the purpose of this lesson is to help the students identify the various services offered by financial institutions and to learn the basics of using a checking account.

TIME REQUIRED
2 class periods.

EXERCISE

A. Ask the students to identify some financial services they use and from what institution they obtain the service. Some students will have savings and checking accounts from commercial banks. Some may even own stocks held at a brokerage firm.

B. Have the students read Exercise 21.1, *What Are Financial Institutions?* in the *Student Workouts*. Ask the students to answer the questions in the exercise. Discuss the answers.

1. Name four common financial institutions. *(Commercial banks, savings and loans, credit unions, and brokerage firms.)*

2. How are financial institutions changing? *(New laws [deregulation] have meant that different financial institutions can now offer similar services.)*

3. What are some of the common deposit services? *(Checking accounts, automated tellers, direct deposits, automatic withdrawals, and deposit insurance.)*

4. What are some of the common credit services? *(Credit cards, installment loans, home equity loans, small business loans.)*

5. What are some common investment services? *(Retirement accounts; financial planning and management of investments; and sales of stocks, bonds, and mutual funds.)*

C. Explain to the class that perhaps checking accounts are the most widely used financial service. Checking accounts make it much easier to pay your bills and have easy access to cash. Direct the students' attention Exercise 21.2, *Checking Out Checking Accounts*, which includes facts about opening and using a checking account. Ask the students to answer the questions at the end of the exercise. Discuss the answers.

1. What is a checking account? *(A checking account allows you to deposit money into an account and then write checks to withdraw money from the account.)*

2. Why do you suppose the signature card is important when you open a checking account? *(The signature card is meant to protect you and the financial institution from unauthorized use of your checking account.)*

103

3. What kind of a checking account is appropriate for most high school students? *(A special account with its service fee and per-check fee is probably the most appropriate for a high school student who does not write many checks.)*

4. What is a blank check endorsement for a check? *(A blank endorsement is simply your signature on the back of the check. This makes the check as good as cash to the holder.)*

5. When should you void a check? *(Void a check when you make a mistake in writing it.)*

6. What is a debit card? *(A debit card allows you to have the amount of a purchase taken directly from your checking account.)*

D. Direct the students' attention to Illustration 21.2, *The Finer Points of Writing a Check.* Explain the different features of the check such as the bank transit routing symbol, bank number, account number, and check number. Explain the parts of the check to be completed by the payer, such as the date line, payee line, amount box, amount line, and so forth. Go over the procedures for writing checks.

E. Have the students turn to Exercise 21.3 and do the transactions in the exercise. Show Visual 21.1 with the completed check register for students to check their work. Have the students exchange checks with one

another to determine whether the checks were written as shown in Illustration 21.2, *The Finer Points of Writing a Check.*

F. Review some of the key points in this lesson. Ask:

1. What are the main financial institution *(Commercial banks, savings and loan associations, credit unions, and brokerage firms.)*

2. List some of the services provided by financial institutions. *(Deposit services, such as checking accounts and savings accounts. Credit services such as credit cards, loans, and mortgages. Investment services, such as retirement accounts, stocks, bonds, and mutual funds.)*

3. What is a checking account? *(A checking account allows you to deposit money into an account and then write checks to withdraw money from the account.)*

4. What does reconciling your checking account mean? *(Reconciling your checkin account means to compare your checkbook register to the monthly statement. Th process includes checking off deposits and withdrawals. Writing the ending balance a shown from the statement, adding deposit in the register but not on the statement, and subtracting withdrawals in the register but not on the statement will allow you to arrive at the adjusted, or correct, balance.)*

COOL DOWN

Direct the students' attention to Exercise 21.4, *Financial Services Summary,* in *Student Workouts* Ask the students to contact local financial institutions to determine the specific services they provide. You may wish to have the students discuss this information with the other members of the class.

Other Training Equipment

An annotated bibliography and Internet resource list are available on our web site, **www.ncee.net**, as well as in *The Parents' Guide to Bringing Home the Gold.*

Visual 21.1

Bank Register Answer Key

PLEASE BE SURE TO DEDUCT CHARGES THAT AFFECT YOUR ACCOUNT

HECK #	DATE	TRANSACTION DESCRIPTION	WITHDRAWAL/ SUBTRACTIONS		✓ T	FEE IF ANY	DEPOSIT/ ADDITIONS		BALANCE	
	3/1	Deposit					250	00	250	00
0994	3/7	CD Sales, Purchased CDs	30	00					220	00
0995	3/8	A. J. Vitullo Company Purchased Sweater	50	00					170	00
0996	3/10	Acme Bicycle Shop, Bicycle Repair	45	10					124	90
0997	3/12	Happy Pets, Pet Supplies	10	00					114	90
	3/14	Gift Money					50	00	164	90
0998	3/16	Lawson School, Purchased 2 basketball tickets	16	00					148	90
0999	3/18	Cash	50	00					98	90

LESSON

22

Managing Risk: The Good News About Insurance

Fitness Focus

EQUIPMENT AND GETTING READY!

✔ Exercise 22.1, *Choices and Risks (Bringing Home the Gold Student Workouts)*

✔ Exercise 22.2, *The Big Risk (Bringing Home the Gold Student Workouts)*

✔ Family Activity 13, *Researching Auto Insurance (The Parents' Guide for Bringing Home the Gold)*

✔ One or two decks of cards with one suit of ace through queen (12 cards) for each small group for use in the Big Risk simulation

LESSON DESCRIPTION

As people begin to acquire assets and an income, they begin to think about how to protect what they have from loss. Toward this end, many people buy insurance. This lesson tells how insurance works and provides an overview of the different types of insurance. Students participate in a simulation that allows them to practice their understanding of the costs and benefits associated with purchasing insurance.

This lesson is correlated with national standards for economics as well as the national guidelines for personal financial management as shown in Tables 1 and 2 in the front of the book.

PARENT CONNECTION

We recommend one family activity worksheet be used with this lesson. Family Activity Worksheet 13 in *The Parents' Guide* encourages your students to comparison shop with their parents for automobile insurance.

The Parents' Guide is a tool for reinforcing and extending the instruction provided in the classroom. It includes:

1. Content background in the form of frequently asked questions.

2. Interesting activities that parents can do with their young adults.

3. An annotated listing of books and Internet resources related to each theme.

Workout

WARM-UP

Explain that the purpose of this lesson is to help the students understand the concept of risk and how the purchase of insurance can help reduce risk. Insurance is usually not regarded as a hot topic, but that may be changing. Debates about how best to provide health insurance to American families not currently covered illustrate its current importance.

EXERCISE

A. Explain that understanding insurance begins with understanding risk. Life is filled with risk. Virtually every decision involves some level of risk. Listening to music on a CD player seems like a low-risk choice. But, it may not be risk-free choice. For example, a hearing loss could result from the very loud volume at which the music is played. Ask:

1. What are some low-risk choices that people make? *(Accept a variety of answers. Some examples of low-risk choices are drinking tap water, eating peanut butter, turning on a light, making a telephone call, taking a walk even though you may be hit by a meteorite.)*

2. What are some high-risk choices that people make? *(Accept a variety of answers. Some examples of high-risk choices are motorcycling, smoking, drinking, using drugs, sport parachuting, hang gliding, and riding bucking broncos.)*

Student Objectives

At the end of this lesson the student will be able to:

✔ Analyze insurance as a way of reducing risk.

✔ Explain that insurance is a way of spreading risk among people in an insurance "pool."

✔ Identify key types of insurance such as health, auto, homeowner's, renter's, life, and disability.

✔ Explain the costs and benefits associated with choices regarding the purchase of insurance.

B. Have the students read Exercise 22.1, *Choices and Risks* in *Student Workouts.* Ask the students to answer the questions at the end of the exercise. Discuss the answers.

1. All choices involve risks. Name two ways to reduce risks. *(First, take steps to reduce risks involving your behavior or your possessions. Second, consider purchasing insurance as way to reduce risks.)*

2. How does insurance work? *(The purpose of insurance is to spread risk over many payers. A pool of people contribute money to buy insurance from an insurance company, with the expectation that only a few of them will actually experience a loss that will need to be covered.)*

3. What is a premium? *(The fee paid for insurance protection.)*

4. What does each type of insurance provide?

a. Auto: *Provides financial protection to the owner, operator, and occupants of an automobile in case of accidents or damages.*

b. Health: *Protects against financial loss due to illness or accident.*

c. Renter's: *Protects the renter from loss due to fire, smoke, or damage to personal possessions.*

d. Homeowner's: *Protects the homeowner from loss due to damage from fire, theft, storms, and so forth.*

e. Life: *Provides financial protection to people who depend on a wage earner when the wage earner dies.*

f. Disability: *Provides income over a specified period when a person is ill or unable to work.*

5. In the case of auto insurance, what is the difference between collision and liability coverage? *(Collision coverage provides for the repair or replacement of the policyholder's car if it is damaged in an accident. Liability protection covers the cost of property damage and injuries to others as a result of an accident.)*

6. In the case of health insurance, what is the difference between basic health and major medical coverage? *(Basic health covers only office visits and routine services. Major medical covers the cost of treatment of catastrophic illness or injury.)*

C. Explain that decisions to buy insurance depend on individual judgments about the future. The general guideline is not to allow a large portion of potential loss to remain uninsured. To illustrate some of the risks associated with choosing or refusing to purchase insurance, the class will participate in a brief simulation. Direct the students' attention to Exercise 22.2, *The Big Risk,* in *Student Workouts.*

D. Divide the class into small groups. Ask the students to imagine that they have just graduated from high school. Select one student in each group who will not insure any of his or her material goods or income; the rest of the group has budgeted $2,600 to purchase insurance.

E. Ask the class to focus on the various risks identified in Exercise 22.2. After the students have examined the possible risks and dollar costs of insuring various things listed, those students who have budgeted money for insurance should decide what insurance they wish to purchase and to circle their choices. Remind them that they may not spend more than $2,600 and may choose to spend less.

F. Demonstrate how to play the game as follows:

1. Distribute one partial suit of cards (ace through queen) to each group. The cards represent the numbers 1-12: ace = 1, 2 = jack = 11, and queen = 12, etc. Ask a student to pull a card from the deck of 12 cards. Look at the number. This number represents the item or items affected by the unexpected events during that particular year. For example, if a "6" is selected the following insurances are affected: automobile, health, and disability (see "card" listing in each insurance box).

2. Instruct the students to locate the "examples" in the exercise titled *Adding Up Insurance.*

3. The first example shows the losses suffered by an uninsured student who drew a "6." The "Loss" category of the insurance boxes lists a $4,600 loss for an automobile accident, $1,200 for medical expenses, and $14,400 for lost wages. The sum is shown in columns 5 and 6. This player has no costs for insurance or deductibles in columns 3 and 4.

4. The second example shows the losses suffered by a person with automobile and disability insurance. The premiums for this insurance ($1,800) are listed in column 3.

Financial Fitness for Life: Bringing Home the Gold Teacher Guide, ©National Council on Economic Education

5. In the fourth column, the deductible or co-pay for each loss should be totaled. Explain that if an item is protected by insurance, the student will pay the deductible or co-payment, if applicable. Explain that a deductible is the portion of the loss that is paid by the insured when the unexpected event happens that is covered by insurance. Since the disability insurance has no deductible, only the $250 for the automobile coverage is included in column 4.

6. The fifth column includes losses that were not insured. No health insurance was purchased so that the health insurance loss of $1,200 would be placed here.

7. The total dollar cost for the person with disability and automobile insurance for the year is noted in column 6 for the second example.

G. Explain that when they play the game the students will not be able to insure all items. Pulling a card from the deck will determine which items will be affected. Uninsured students will experience losses in all categories affected by pulling a card from the deck.

H. Play the simulation. The simulation represents five years. Have a student in each group pull a card five times. Shuffle the cards before choosing one for each year. At the end of the five years, students should

calculate the total amount spent for the five-year period. Discuss what the students learned. Ask:

1. Which students had fewer losses? (*Students who had purchased insurance.*)

2. Were the costs of purchasing insurance worth the benefits? (*Yes. In most cases students who purchased insurance were better off than those who did not.*)

I. Review some of the key points in this lesson. Ask:

1. How does insurance work? (*The idea of insurance is to spread a risk over many payers. A pool of people contribute money to buy insurance from an insurance company with the expectation that only a few will actually experience a loss that will need to be covered.*)

2. What is a premium? Deductible? (*A premium is the fee paid for insurance protection. A deductible is the amount of loss paid by the insured.*)

3. What types of insurance are commonly available? (*Auto, health, renter's, homeowner's, life, disability.*)

4. Is the cost of buying insurance worth the benefit? (*Accept a variety of answers but stress the general guideline that it is not wise to let a large portion of potential loss remain uninsured.*)

COOL DOWN

Ask a small group of students to call local insurance brokers or use the Internet to find information about auto insurance. The students should find out how much it would cost them to purchase auto insurance. They will learn that answers will vary depending upon the students' driving record, type of car, age of car, present grades, completion of drivers' education, what coverage is sought, and so forth. Ask the students to report the results to the class.

Other Training Equipment

An annotated bibliography and Internet resource list are available on our web site, **www.ncee.net**, as well as in *The Parents' Guide to Bringing Home the Gold*.

Notes

NOTES